Guns and Boyhood in America

POETS ON POETRY

DAVID LEHMAN, GENERAL EDITOR

DONALD HALL, FOUNDING EDITOR

Jonathan Holden

Guns and Boyhood in America

**A MEMOIR
OF GROWING UP
IN THE 50s**

Ann Arbor

THE UNIVERSITY OF MICHIGAN PRESS

2000   1999   1998   1997   4   3   2   1

A CIP catalog record for this book is available from the British Library.

Library of Congress Cataloging-in-Publication Data

Holden, Jonathan.
    Guns and boyhood in America : a memoir of growing up in
    the 50s / Jonathan Holden.
        p.   cm.—(Poets on poetry)
    ISBN 0-472-09643-5 (cloth)   0-472-06643-9 (paper)
    1. Holden, Jonathan—Homes and haunts—New Jersey.
2. Poets, American—20th century—Biography. 3. Holden,
Jonathan—Childhood and youth. 4. New Jersey—Social life
and customs. 5. Boys—United States. I. Title. II. Series.
PS3558.034775Z47 1997
811'.54—dc21
    [B]   96-49137
                                                        CIP

An American Boyhood

There was little important
to do but chew gum, or count
the ways a flipped jackknife
caught in the dirt.
One Sunday afternoon I had an idea.
We clamped the cables of Tommy
Emory's train transformer
to a steel pie plate
filled with saltwater
and drank through our fingers
the current's purr,
dialing that bird-heartbeat
higher, riding its flutter until
both hands were bucked
out of water.
                            We knew
we were wasting our time,
though we had nothing
but time. Our parents
moved vague among their great
worries, remote
as the imperatives of weather.
And the stars appeared on schedule
to run their dim, high errands
again, leaving us lost
in the long boredom of our childhood,
flipping our knives in the dust,
waiting to find out just how
in this world we were going
to be necessary.

Contents

Guns and Boyhood in America

Introduction

It is conventional wisdom, I guess, that a person's aesthetic inclinations spring from childhood experience. "The child is the father of the man," Wordsworth proclaimed, and certainly one of the best and most enduring testaments to this truth is *The Prelude,* where Wordsworth describes some of the most vivid moments of his boyhood—scaling a cliff to pilfer eggs from a bird's nest; unmooring somebody else's boat and rowing it out into the middle of a lake to get a different view of things; leaving a hockey game at dusk to skate alone, to be alone with his own thoughts. In book 12 of *The Prelude,* he writes:

> There are in our existence spots of time,
> That with distinct pre-eminence retain
> A renovating virtue, whence, depressed
> By false opinion and contentious thought,
> Or aught of heavier or more deadly weight,
> In trivial occupations, and the round
> Of ordinary intercourse, our minds
> Are nourished and invisibly repaired.

The passage above, like much Romantic literature, verges on sentimentality. The type of boyhood that Wordsworth describes is virtually impossible to lead now, in England or anywhere in Europe, unless one is a billionaire, able literally to buy a tract of nature for one's own private use. When hiking in Interlaken, Switzerland, or around Lake Como on a fair summer's day, it is next to impossible to find even the slightest nook or cranny that isn't teeming with other humans. A rock is like a park bench. A tree is like a public beach umbrella. The Alps, for all their scale, the gray fangs and sinister silence of their glaciers, resemble a melodramatic stage set.

In America, as in Europe, nature is a stage set, but for a different kind of script. Here, when there are woods around, they're the stage set for acting out fantasies about cowboys, six-shooters, Indians, outlaws, hideouts, ambushes, being quick on the draw. In the woods near my parents' house in what was then rural New Jersey, I indulged in a menu of typical boyhood fantasies. But my boyhood was not typical. I was born an identical twin. My brother Stephen, genetically identical to me, was somehow different from me—radically different—though it was not until I was nineteen years old that I found out what the difference was: that he was homosexual and I was not. And it was only much later, in middle age, after my miserable twenty-seven-year marriage came apart, that with the help of psychotherapy I began to see how desperately and extremely I had twisted myself in order to play a role that I thought was safe and acceptable: to be a pleasant, self-effacing guy with a blond crew cut, shy, boyish—a guy who was such an expert at what he did that, like my father, Alan, who was a scientist, I could dispense with the inconvenience of an inner life; for I believed that to be a successful grown-up meant you didn't feel much. Grown-ups, I was positive, lived without too much emotional distraction, and I was positive I would be able to know when I had arrived at that condition.

ぇ

Stephen and I were born in All Souls Hospital, in Morristown, New Jersey, on July 18, 1941. We were tiny. We barely escaped the incubator.

All of our childhood was spent in New Jersey, in a renovated farmhouse on seven acres on Pleasantville Road bordering the Great Swamp thirty miles west of the Holland Tunnel. Our father, Alan, who had graduated summa cum laude with a B.S. in chemistry from Harvard in 1925, worked as a physical chemist for the Bell Telephone Laboratories in Murray Hill, New Jersey. My mother, Jaynet, was a typical scientist's wife—and in the context of the Bell labs, a model corporation

wife—cooking for Alan, cleaning for him, typing his manu-
scripts, entertaining his illustrious friends, making certain he
had time and space to work.

Alan was a heavy smoker, and for the last several years, he
was all but immobilized by emphysema. One day, in August
1985, he began to choke on his own mucus. The local emer-
gency squad was summoned, and they tried to pump out his
lungs. The stress on his body was too great. His heart gave
out. A month later, Jaynet was found fully dressed, dead on
the piano-room couch. She had, several years earlier, been
stricken with a form of cancer called multiple myeloma. Everybody who knew Alan and Jaynet assumed that she had kept
herself alive to see Alan through to the end. She may have
died by her own hand. Jaynet was a lady of unusual passion
and determination, and, in her final days, incredible courage.
At the memorial service, all those assembled agreed that
Jaynet and Alan's marriage had been one "made in heaven."
For fifty years, they had been in love with each other, absorbed with each other, leaving Stephen and me to fend
largely for ourselves.

In the late 1940s and early 1950s, five miles from the nearest town, there were few other children to play with. We had
no television. Alan was remote. He spent most weekends
seated at the dining room table, doing mathematics. Each of
us had literally to invent boyhood on his own, to construct it as
he went along. I constructed mine around baseball and, to a
lesser extent, around airplanes and various military fantasies.
I assembled the biggest collection of cap pistols and airplane
books on Pleasantville Road. Stephen constructed his boyhood around popular music over the radio and dreams of
Hollywood. He collected copies of *Photoplay*.

Jaynet, though not interested in Hollywood, had a romantic nature, and she encouraged Stephen's interest in piano
and acting—in stardom. Although it was not until high school
that I became fully aware of the dangers of being seen as
"feminine" as a boy in America, sometime around third grade
I began to distance myself from Stephen. We began to lead
parallel lives, mine outdoors in the woods with the few boys
on Pleasantville, he upstairs in his room by the radio.

In America, the officially sanctioned outlet for a boy's aesthetic nature is sports. In the 1950s, outlets like piano or ballet compromised a boy's masculine reputation. Piano was especially suspect, partly because of the fame of the late Liberace. From Liberace, I think, may have derived the stigma of a boy's having long hair—of being "a longhair"—but the figure of Liberace is an icon that could only have been invented by a country that sneers at the feminine in men as routinely as most Americans still do:

Liberace

It took generations to mature
this figure. Every day it
had to be caught sneaking off
to its piano lesson and beaten up.
Every day it came back
for more. It would have been
trampled underground, but
like a drop of mercury, it was
too slippery. Stamped on,
it would divide, squirt away
and gather somewhere else, it was
insoluble, it had nowhere to go.
All it could do was gather again,
a puddle in the desert, festering
until the water had gone punk, it
was no good for anything anymore.
It wears rubies on its fingers now.
Between its dimples, its leer is
fixed. Its cheeks are
chocked, its eyes twinkle, it
knows. Thank you, it breathes
with ointment in its voice,
Thank you very much.

In America, the feminine side of men is under such unremitting assault, is so constantly harassed that, despite the Gay

Liberation Movement, in most places and certainly where I live in Kansas, it is still "underground"—queer. The queer is both suppressed and repressed, and the structure of this book reflects that fact. Except for the chapters "Tea and Sympathy" and "American Anaesthetics," with its horrifying memory of my own mistreatment of Stephen, I write as though Stephen didn't exist. Yet there's a sense in which the entire book is about him.

The structure of *Guns and Boyhood in America* yields, implicitly, a second, invidious meaning from the very word *boyhood:* "*Artificial* Aesthetics," "*Compensatory* Aesthetics," "*Homophobic* Aesthetics," "*Ur-Fascist* Aesthetics." What are most of the chapters about? The beauty of military planes, the beauty of guns and gunshot noises, the allure of fistfights (and military adventures), the allure of Los Alamos and Trinity to the physicists I was raised among. In its repression of the theme of Stephen, and in its almost boastful description and celebration of stereotypically boyhood activities, this book exhibits, I note, with wry unsurprise, a perfect duality.

It is also dismaying, in reviewing these chapters, to see how profoundly *military* my aesthetic life as a boy was, even though I never served in the army. It shouldn't be surprising, I guess. Born in 1941, I was a "war baby." My entire boyhood was spent under the shadow of the Cold War and, from the age of five on, lived in the culture of implicit nuclear terror. Everything in our lives was contaminated by it. As the physicist J. Robert Oppenheimer famously declared, about the Trinity blast: "We knew the world would not be the same."

My father's livelihood was conditioned by Trinity: He was a physical chemist. The comfortable circumstances I was raised in were made possible by war. If there is one theme that unites these chapters beyond their implicit homophobia, and their forced construction of a stereotypical boyhood with its fixation on guns, airplanes, and baseball, it would be the grimness of their aesthetics. In America, to satisfy the human tropism to beauty, we are driven to seek glints of it in unlikely places, strike chips of it off surfaces of steel, cement. Dr. Williams was talking not only about New Jersey when he counseled:

> —through metaphor to reconcile
> the people and the stones.
> Compose. (No ideas
> but in things) Invent!
> Saxifrage is my flower that splits
> the rocks.

He was talking about aesthetic survival in America.

Perhaps the darkest chapter in this book is one that, if I wrote it, would be titled "The End of Boyhood." It would describe how, at the age of fifty, I left my marriage and, for the first time ever, like an eighteen-year-old going off to college, set up a life on my own. The dark part would not be the divorce, which was long overdue. The dark part would be that, as is the case with most American men in the middle class, I was spoiled: my boyhood had been protracted into middle age. I never wanted or even intended to grow up; for I could see from early on that to grow up meant going to work—doing *real* work. From the age of around twenty-two, after getting a taste of real work and hating it, I resolved to try to structure my life aesthetically.

Stephen and I had been taught by Alan that the ideal life was one in which you made your living, as he did, doing something you loved, in which "work" was like play. Robert Frost had said it best in "Two Tramps in Mud Time":

> But yield who will to their separation,
> My object in living is to unite
> My avocation and my vocation
> As my two eyes make one in sight.

A defiant ideal, I think—outrageous when you stop to think about it, especially the words "My object in living." "My object in living" is to play. What Frost, the first "poet-in-residence" in the United States, at Amherst College and at the University of Michigan, found was what I and many other writers have since found, that colleges and universities are ideal venues for "play," for the kind of serious intellectual exercise that creative writing is.

Sometimes, on a weekday morning when I'm at home writing, but have contracted for a plumber or a carpenter to do work on my house, as the guy bends to the job downstairs while I sit upstairs in front of my computer, the luxury of spending entire mornings writing seems so unfair that I wonder what the man working furiously away downstairs must wonder about me: "What does this guy do all day?" and a corollary question, "Why does he get his mornings off and not me?" My hypothetical dialogue has this ending: "Why do I get to spend the morning up here by myself, toying around, while you have to do real work to make a living? The answer is simple: I did well in school." But I feel some chagrin. I remember how, in the halls of Morristown High School in the late 1950s, I used to stay discreetly out of the path of certain working-class kids, and of my dread of being mistaken for Stephen. The two anxieties were connected. In Morristown High, Stephen was conspicuous, like Oscar Wilde visiting Leadville, Colorado. The gang that is always there, in the halls of every public high school, had sniffed out Stephen's femininity: his aesthetic nature. It was blood for sharks. Wasn't it?

Although born with a highly aesthetic nature, I had gone far out of my way to conceal my extreme sensitivity: I had trashed it. In a poem called "The Men in the Hoboken Bar," I describe, better than I could in prose, my unease.

> The men in the Hoboken bar
> don't give you a second
> glance as you walk in,
> they figure you're one of
> them, in hiding,
> another bulge in the dim
> *bas relief* of a bar.
> But I watch them—how they talk
> too loud. How they
> shoulder space aside
> as if it got in their way.
> How they do this to cover up
> some faint chagrin,
> like men whose weapons
> have been taken from them.

And I think how when you're a boy
when simply to pick up a stick
and whack a tree
you do for its own sake,
you believe the self-pitying way
a father loosens his tie
at the end of the day
or downs like a casual expletive
his slug of whisky and wipes
his lips on his sleeve
are gestures you practice.
His face never looked this
sad, rumpled
as the heavy suits these men
consent to wear home,
so in need of ironing.
My ambition was to be here, one
of them. I wanted only
to be used. I believed
in the secret company of men.

And now we're all here
refrigerated far indoors
out of the heat of rush-hour.
As I watch them joshing
each other, fooled by their own
suits, the tough on their faces
an expensive cosmetic
already cracking up,
what I see is organized self-pity,
and I'm glad it is dark.
If they suspected, they'd look
at me hard, the way a man's supposed
to look at a girl, at only
the body—to screw it
or beat it up
is all the same to him.
And I wipe my lips on my sleeve,
get up and slip through.

When at last I graduated from high school, I felt an immense relief. It was as if I had been serving time in a penitentiary, under constant threat of bodily harm. Now I could pursue an education without being afraid. I'd gotten away, I'd slipped through. But at what cost? Inauthenticity—a persona so artificial, so twisted that it might never be straightened out. Yet wasn't this the case for most American men? Hadn't we been trained to be assertive, to look more confident and masterful than we felt—trained in bravado? Trained to not sniffle? Trained to hide our feelings? In 1988, I wrote a poem exploring these issues. It's a poem that, I can see now, is the fraternal twin of "Liberace."

Cowboy

At dawn he dressed for his job
and broke in the heavy implements
that made a man of him—
saddle for armchair, horse for a bride,
the beaten, impermeable boots
of his words—*Kiss my ass!*
Step over that line. I dare you.
He learned how to ride always away,
how, in the desert alone,
if he rode faithfully toward the horizon
the skyline would keep its distance from him.
He picked up a stoical set to the jaw,
useful, he thought, as a shovel, a knife.
It drove the barmaids in Dodge City
half crazy to people that void with themselves.
And their false, lip-sticked faces
were mirrors for him.
He could scarcely tear his gaze
away from them.
Every face was a theatre of grief.

From girl he would gallop to girl,
searching the painted jails of their eyes

for the one he would rescue—
a fairy captive in rouge.
All week the furious tromp of his boots
as he'd burst into the town saloon.
With every squirt of his
that hit the spitoon
her existence was officially denied
except on Friday nights.
Late, always after too many drinks,
he could find her again.
He'd hurt her, then hang his head,
and shamble there, awkward, at the foot
of the bed, letting the tears,
paroled at last, roll freely out.
It disarmed him when she would cry like that.
He hated a woman's crying, he said.
And when nothing he could say did any good,
satisfied, he'd tuck in his shirt.
He was free now to pull back on his boots,
free to saddle up, free to ride away
to his job and on toward the skyline.

In high school and long after that, it had seemed necessary—
a sort of survival technique—to proclaim conspicuously to the
world my contempt of "faggots," "fairies," anything conspicuously "soft" in a man, and to identify convenient scapegoats.
The figure of Liberace was a convenient public scapegoat; but
in grade school and in high school we found immediate ones.
We were like a mob, and every mob needs a scapegoat: that
figure identified by anthropologists as the *Pharmakos*.

Who were they? Who are they? The women we've hurt.
The homosexuals we've joked about. My own identical twin
brother. And therefore (of course), as G. Legman points out in
The Rationale of the Dirty Joke, ourselves. In the mid-1990s in
America, in order to write with an emotional honesty that is
credible, it is necessary to entertain the possibility of human
beings having a bisexual nature, whether they admit to it or

not. The Cowboy who is the protagonist of my poem, "Cowboy," lives where we live, "in the desert alone"—the same country that Ezra Pound in *Mauberley* had so matter-of-factly labeled "half savage."

In the following chapters, I follow this Cowboy's tracks as he continues faithfully toward the horizon.

I

Guns and Boyhood
in America

Guns and Boyhood in America

For me, as a boy, certainly the most beautiful sound in the world, more beautiful than Mozart or Bach, was the sound of an explosion—the report of a firecracker or a rifle shot. I studied such sounds—their complicated, collapsing echoes—in the vain hope that I could capture them by somehow repro-ducing them, either with my own palate and saliva (Kkkkk!) when playing with Tommy Emory, Jimmy Connon, and the other neighborhood kids the open-ended game that we called "Guns," or by some kind of word, some verbal expletive like BANG. If I'd been allowed by my parents to own and shoot guns, or if such magical entities as firecrackers had been legal in New Jersey and therefore readily available, I probably wouldn't have dwelt upon such sounds in the almost prurient way that I did—and that, if my thirteen-year-old son and his pals are any indication, most American boys are doing still, have probably always done. But we were forbidden by state law (in my case, also by parental law) from indulging in the expediency of the literal, so we had to go to almost fantastic trouble to steal little voyeuristic peeks into those flash/bang mysteries that, on the radio and in comic books and movies, were so ubiquitous that shooting seemed part of the American landscape itself. It was the Colt .45 six-shooter, after all, that had "won" the West, had secured for us our ongoing day-dream of boyhood paradise—that ideal "territory," the fron-tier, for which Huck Finn had once lit out. We sensed, all of us, that if one were born American and male, then mastery of

From the *Georgia Review,* Summer 1988.

such sounds, together with ownership and control of the machinery to make them, was our birthright.

I and the other boys on Pleasantville Road prepared regularly, systematically almost, to lay claim to this birthright. We prepared for it after school as well as on weekends and, of course, all summer, every afternoon. We prepared for it with the same unquestioning seriousness with which we made revving noises as we pushed toy dump trucks and toy bulldozers through the sand, the same, unquestioning fervency with which Pat Burke's four sisters played with dolls. We even practiced being wounded by gunshots—grunting, staggering back, and doubling up, finally to crumple to the lawn the way they did it in the movies. I don't know whether or not little boys in Europe do this; but neither time that I've been there have I ever noticed kids playing "guns." Maybe, after two world wars, they've had enough. Maybe playing "guns" is no fun for them anymore. But as an American boy, playing in a countryside that has never been invaded, I felt sanctimonious—a kind of deep solemnity—when Tommy Emory or Pat Burke would make a gunshot noise and I decided to be wounded, and so would clutch my arm and fall. Sometimes I would emit low moans. When dying in make-believe, I felt suddenly like a grown-up. Somebody had to pretend to be dead. Although it was not a glamorous role, I would do it for the others. And the role had its charms—subtle ones. I think I imagined being wounded as like being sick. Whenever I had to stay home from school with a headache or a sore throat, and my mother took my temperature and smoothed my brow and spoiled me, placing tall glasses of chocolate milk beside my bed, I became dramatically, incontestably important.

I had fifteen cap pistols of various kinds. The more of them I bought, the more particular I got. I demanded realism. A toy handgun had to pass two criteria. It had to resemble physically any of the countless pistols I had seen in movies or that I mooned over in the sporting-goods section of the Sears catalog. And it had to produce audio or visual phenomena like those of a real gun. All of us boys squandered our allowances on rolls of caps as readily as, years later, we'd spend our money on beer. But caps were never loud enough to shock us the way we wanted to be shocked, unless you placed a whole new roll on the flagstone by the back door and flattened it with a framing hammer. The most imaginative cap pistol I owned was a pretty good replica of a Colt .45. It was called a ".45 Smoker," and it had a little door in one side. You'd open the door, pour flour or cornstarch in, shut it again. When the toy was thus loaded, the barrel would emit pale puffs of cornstarch dust when you fanned the hammer.

One day, for reasons I don't recall, I lit a candle and was fanning the hammer furiously, volleying puffs into the candle flame, when to my astonishment, there was a low "whoosh!" and a modest fireball rolled out. I repeated this experiment successfully enough times that it became predictable. The fireball was a measly one anyway, so I cut a two-foot length from a garden hose, poured some cornstarch into one end, held it up to the candle, and blew. My first try blew the candle out, but finally, through persistent trial and error, I produced some larger "whooshes."

It's in the nature of pyrotechnic play that as the limit of each stage of development is reached, it gets familiar and thus boring. The play's addictive, and a player is continuously, inexorably tempted toward trying to make a bigger bang—something that will truly surprise him—a BANG big enough to sober him up once and for all.

My father was a physical chemist at the Bell Telephone labs in Murray Hill. To encourage my interest in science, my parents got me, one Christmas, a Gilbert Chemistry Set. Most of the experiments in the little manual looked boring, but one stood out: a recipe for gunpowder, the first and only chemical experiment that ever interested me. It called for the classic ingredients: potassium nitrate, sulfur, and powdered charcoal. I don't remember the proportions, but I do remember looking up "Gunpowder" in *The Encyclopaedia Britannica* and learning that many different proportions had been tried over hundreds of years, as if civilization itself had always been composed of bloodthirsty little boys scheming together, conducting experiments about how to make the biggest bang. The residents of ancient China had been every bit as absorbed in the problem as we were in A.D. 1955 in New Jersey.

The encyclopedia entry on gunpowder was my first inkling that every single one of the destructive arts that so fascinated us as boys had equally fascinated ancient peoples. Such arts, when they didn't require any modern technology—I learned this later when studying karate—had been perfected thousands of years ago. Young men had thought up every possible method of dirty fighting (apparently one of the first things so-called civilized people worried about), and they refined these methods and the means of teaching them en masse to soldiers so efficiently that no more improvement, no further "progress" in the art was possible.

As I stared at the pitifully small bottle of saltpeter provided me by the Gilbert Chemistry Set, almost my first thought was how to get more. Order another whole chemistry set to get one bottle? The problem of how to get saltpeter, though I didn't know it then, also had a history. As gunpowder became known and (of course, popular) in Europe, old barns and old buildings—all places where bird-droppings had accumulated conspicuously—were scoured for the precious substance, just as landscapes are scoured for uranium today.

The gunpowder I made was a disappointment. It fizzled meekly. So, for a bang, I fell back on the staple I was used to, kitchen matches. I'd found that if I whanged Ohio Blue Tips with a hammer on the back-door flagstone, the match-head might emit a little snap. Science is a collective enterprise. It had been discovered by us neighborhood boys that the pale blue pimple at the tip of a kitchen match was the magic part, providing initial ignition, which would spread down through the slower-igniting navy blue crust that jacketed the rest of the match-head. On a kitchen cutting board, over a sheet of crisp, new typing paper creased by a single fold along which I could jiggle into an empty aspirin bottle any random scraps of the phosphorescent tips, using my mother's best kitchen knife we'd saw or else chop the live tips off the matches, hundreds of them, boxes of them. We worked with the purposeful patience of adults. Then, because we'd been taught to be neat and always pick up after ourselves, we'd throw the useless sticks, like the stripped carcasses of so many tiny wooden chickens, into the garbage.

Not only would the match-tips snap when smashed. They flared with enough gusto that, perhaps, you could use them to fuel a rocket or to make your own cannon cracker. But these projects failed. The rockets I designed out of rolled typing paper, when tilted heavenward inside a launcher of galvanized stovepipe and then set off, strained to move, to overcome friction as they flared, full of brief hope, before the propellant fizzled, leaving the little paper husk like a stranded car burning peacefully. There were also formidable problems in the design of match-head bombs, not unlike an engineering problem faced in World War I: how to synchronize the fire of a cockpit machine gun with the monoplane's propeller so that in a dogfight the pilot could shoot straight ahead without shooting his own propeller off. You had to have a fuse that would pass through the seal to the explosive without either destroying the seal or going out.

In his charming memoir, *Surely You're Joking, Mr. Feynman,* the Nobel Prize–winning physicist Richard Feynman describes the difference between science and superstition, proposing a concept that he calls "Cargo Cult Science":

> In the South Seas there is a cargo cult of people. During the war they saw airplanes land with lots of good materials, and they want to make the same thing happen now. So they've arranged to make things like runways, to put fires along the sides of the runways, to make a wooden hut for a man to sit in, with two pieces on his head like headphones and bars of bamboo sticking out like antenna—he's the controller—and they wait for the airplanes to land. They're doing everything right. The form is perfect. It looks exactly the way it looked before. But it doesn't work. No airplanes land.

Like the South Sea Islanders Feynman describes, we were ignorant of the principles that go into making a good fuse; but we knew what a fuse should look like. We'd seen them in the movies and firsthand when we were lucky enough to handle the few real fireworks our buddies smuggled into New Jersey. Fuses looked a lot like string, so we tried string. But the string did not burn with a hiss. It didn't progress grimly toward its destination with the sparkling intensity of any of the Hollywood fuses we'd seen eating their way toward a powder keg. To be sure, they *looked* like fuses, like tails of demons snaking out of cylinders, coiling along the ground with ominous portent. But when we lit them, an inch or so of string would burn, and the ash would break off, leaving the rest of the string dormant, inert—just a length of stupid household string.

My father mistook my experiments with gunpowder for an interest in science, and he made a dangerous mistake. To encourage me, he brought back from the labs a bottle of potassium nitrate (KNO_3), and when I *still* couldn't make lively enough gunpowder, he brought back a bottle of potassium chlorate ($KClO_3$). As he knew, $KClO_3$ was a much more efficient and faster oxidizing agent than KNO_3. Father, who was a good chemist and had developed a crystal used in sonar anti-submarine detection in World War II, had the sense to warn me that whereas grinding the three ingredients for gunpowder together with the back of a tablespoon was probably not too dangerous when using KNO_3, he wouldn't advise doing that with $KClO_3$. So I poured the powders together into a little cardboard box that, a Christmas before, had housed my first tie-clip, taking care to pluck out the cotton lining and save it for bomb-seals. Then I fit the lid back on, squeezed tight, and shook. The final mixture was an unnatural grayish green, the same color we see in the backdrop to the line-squall of a really ugly thunderstorm as it rolls up over the trees—and it proved to burn much faster than the old. But I still couldn't get it to go off by hitting it. Because of the fuse problem, I still couldn't make a bomb that would explode.

But my determination was undiminished. Our neighbors, the Walters, had built a shooting range up in the woods. It was only a few hundred yards away, and sometimes on a Saturday or Sunday we could hear, for an hour or so, the tantalizing echo of a .22 tear again and again through those rickety woods. It was a mysterious sound, because it was many possible sounds at once: it was as if somebody had dropped an armload of dry shingles; it was as if some ghostly express train were racing through the trees at an impossible speed, going east and west at the same time. The thin, dry echoes bristled from different points at once. Now and then, when I heard the shooting start, I'd wander up the bridle path to the clearing where old Fred Walter and his son, Richard, had set up their range—a wall of railroad ties backed by dirt. I'd just stand there with the hangdog, solemn politeness of a little boy requesting candy, a boy embarrassed by the obviousness of his own greed but determined to cover it. I'd stand there whiffing the blue tang of the gunsmoke (the scent seemed as elusive and full of longing as the color blue itself, full of adult seriousness and withheld knowledge), and I'd muse upon the heft and texture and force of each shot, trying to gauge it, trying not so much to understand it as to get a sense of it, and loving almost as much as the stroke of each shot the complex clack of the rifle's bolt action ejecting a shell—loving, as I put it years later in a poem:

> that slick, exact way
> the steel sleeves of the breech
> unlock, retract, consolidate
> shut . . .

The Walters left the shells in the dirt where they landed. I would collect them and take them home. I had found a use for them.

There was a way around the "fuse problem." You could fill the brass shell of a .22-long about half full of my improved potassium chlorate powder and pack the end with cotton. Then you could take a full double-page from the classified section of the Sunday *New York Times,* place the .22 shell on it, bunch the paper around it into a loose ball, place this ball out on the ash patch near the defunct corncrib where my family burned brush, and apply a match. A modest cage of flame would engulf the shell, heating it up until: Eureka!

One summer afternoon Jaynet was weeding the family garden about thirty feet southeast of my little proving ground, where I was conducting another test. As she bent to grip a weed, CRACK! the bomb test succeeded, and something sang past her left ear. That afternoon marked the end of my supply of chemicals.

In an effort to grasp more fully the gunshot sounds I pined for, I studied and evaluated the words for these sounds in the hundreds of comic books I owned. I studied them as seriously as I studied and rehearsed Stan "The Man" Musial's coiled, stealthy batting stance, as if Musial were peeking around a corner. The basic formulas, BANG! CRACK! POW! BAM! BLAM! and RAT-A-TAT-TAT! I thought to be wholly inadequate. They weren't especially accurate. They didn't capture the mysterious essence of a shot. They were clichés. I vowed that when I became a comic-book artist I would give serious attention to this matter. I would correct the problem.

Our neighbors the Remsens had visited Belgium, and the Remsen boys, Tony and Derek, brought back a Belgian comic-book version of the Red Rider. The text was in French, and the report of a rifle was denoted by the word "PAN!" Not knowing any French, I didn't know enough to nasalize the pronunciation, to omit the *n* sound; but even had I known enough to do that, I would have found the result, "P-agh!" inadequate. It didn't capture the elusive beauty of echoes. (I was rehashing these issues with the poet Robert Pinsky, who proposed an enviable invention, one that, thirty years ago, I would have used dozens of times a day. He pointed out that POW! could be improved with an extra *P* hyphenated as a prefix: P-POW!—a sophisticated improvement on the KA-POW! of the Walters' .22 shots in the woods, shots far enough away that the echo reached you before the initial report. P-POW! put one right up at the shooting range again.)

In the early 1950s there was one comic book that not only took seriously the sounds of specific gunshots but also took pains to represent weapons, uniforms, planes, and all other military equipment, with documentary accuracy. This was *Two-Fisted Tales*, a war comic from a line of comics that, for aficionados, has become legendary: E.C. Comics, edited by William M. Gaines. *Two-Fisted Tales* presented mainly Korean War stories. But, unlike other comics, it wasn't propagandistic. It didn't present war as fantasy. It wasn't, like *G.I. Joe*, nostalgic. It was realistic in its presentation of war, and its tone was, if anything, ironic. *Two-Fisted Tales* depicted mortars that went PONG! and PONK! When the Red Chinese infantry assaulted American GIs in human waves, the Communist submachine guns, known as "burp guns," emitted a noise that I had never seen in a comic before, a nasty BRRRR-APPP!

As the Korean War ended, *Two-Fisted Tales* looked for new material, and, needing a war, began depicting famous battles from history—especially Civil War battles. As usual, the illustrators took pains to render everything—climate, topography, uniforms, and weapons—with documentary authenticity. I remember two episodes in particular. The duel between the Monitor and the Merrimack was memorable because it was there I learned that cannonballs could be skipped like stones over great spans of water. The other was "The Battle of Lexington and Concord," as presented by the artist Al Williamson. Williamson came up with the single best gunshot noise I have ever encountered, in comics or out. As the front rank of British regulars marched in cadence toward the Colonists (who were crouched behind a low, crumbling stone wall, waiting until, as our Social Studies teacher said, they could "see the whites of their eyes"), Williamson's task was to come up with a word for the voluptuous sound of a fusillade of flintlocks and matchlocks. He did, and I remember it virtually letter by letter: FAP! PAD-A-BOW!

One of the comic-book gunshot sounds that I'd dismissed at the time as a cliché was much more accurate than I had realized. It was thirty years later, after firing a .357 magnum at a limestone outcrop, that I discovered how seriously I had underrated BAM! "BAM!" is almost exactly the sound a magnum makes. BAM! As both your hands lift off, the blast not only leaves your ears ringing, it seems almost to numb the entire right hemisphere of your head. It *is*, as the cliché would have it, "ear-splitting." I'd shot a .22 revolver once, but never a handgun of this horsepower. I found it amazing.

Most new experiences, if they pack any wallop—any danger or fear or guilt—retain a certain mysteriousness until one gets used to them. It's this mysteriousness that calls one back to replay them, to dwell upon them. The most artful way of dwelling on such elusive moments is verbal—by trying to describe them in words, adjusting the words in tiny, hair-splitting ways as if with calipers until they fit the experience exactly. To get the right fit, to "capture" the experience, is one reason people practice "creative writing," but it's not the main one. The main one is that as one is indulging in the serious playfulness of trying to find "the right words," one comes to learn much more about the essence of the experience than one had expected. The great, implicit axiom that underlies imaginative writing is the plausible assumption that the only way to begin to understand matters of any subtlety is to tinker around with possible words for them. Good writing is a heuristic method of investigation.

Even before I tried to describe shooting the magnum, I knew that everything I'd ever heard about Americans and guns, like H. Rap Brown's infamous dictum, "Violence is American as apple pie," was true. But until I started writing, what I knew—and believed—had only the force of a truism; as I envisioned curling my fingers around the handle of the magnum, I recalled the feel of all the cap pistols I'd used to tote as a boy. My whole, trigger-happy boyhood began to crystallize again, and I understood with real force and with a sudden chagrin, just how profoundly and insidiously my own boyhood aesthetic fascination with guns was implicated in the very fabric of American culture and history.

I thought back to the times I had pretended to be wounded by gunfire as a boy, to the corny swoon I entertained as I would topple to the grass and lie, moaning, waiting for some maternal nurse to descend and fuss over me. And I realized: This is how boys in America are encouraged—from the moment they're handed their first, plastic, toy automatic (Mattel Corporation manufactures the stock for the M16)—to give their bodies to the military. Combat is presented to them as exciting and beautiful, pain as make-believe. I thought of how thoroughly weaponry is woven into the American landscape itself, so ubiquitous that we scarcely notice it. Where I live, the daily artillery practice fifteen miles away at Ft. Riley is fitful summer thunder, weekday hatching of malefaction acknowledged only once a year, on the Fourth of July.

I think that it's mainly because, in movies and on TV, gun-fighting is presented with an aesthetic veneer—as the natural, manly way to conduct a dispute—that the average, middle-class American accepts the condition of living in such a heavily armed environment. But the presentation of guns as aesthetic is a seductive lie. I once saw handguns used in a civilian argument that validated James Dickey's *Deliverance* as anything but fantasy. The incident took place on a canoe trip in southeastern Missouri, when one of our party got into an argument with two rednecks known as the Brown Brothers who lived in a trailer overlooking Courteois Creek. I drew on the experience later, near the end of a poem of mine called "River Time":

And two men, two fat retarded twins
in bib-overalls, two comical men,
humpty-dumpties with rotted mouths
were circling my Minnesota friend,
spitting words, gesticulating at him,
arguing he better move his goddam
hippie van because this floodplain
here belonged to *them,* while Tom,
from the cab, glared down with a stiff
slightly puzzled stare, white-knuckled
in the face. And the look the architect
slipped me meant something dirty
he knew about, it meant *Move off.*
We walked our canoe across the ford,
shoved it up on mud. The rain
returned, through the rain
we watched one brother squat
behind Tom's camper to jot the plate.
Tom's truck wallowed, bucking in reverse
like a dog digging, spewing back rocks.
But the fat guy expected it. He lurched
the gap to his pick-up's cab,
and the long .22 automatic he pulled
discharged its six dried-twig snaps
at the back where Tom's boy bounced
as the rear of the fleeing camper
leapt over the crest and out of sight.

In fistfights the hate-scent can be so strong
it gets the tightening circle half incensed.
But anger, in a shot, goes so abstract
at first you can't even recognize it.
Just this detached small-kindling spark.
Could it be some practical joke
over which both brothers on the opposite bank
now chortled and whooped like Laurel and Hardy,
they were slapping their knees, congratulating
each other with whops on the back. *What time
was it?* All I knew was how wet and cold
and pathetic we looked, searching
for footholds in the mud, slipping,
digging in our heels again and heaving
our canoes up the bank—
how sick of this desolate river and the rain.

There was an ugly, aimless quality to the scene. The *snaps*
of the shots sounded trivial. The Brown Brothers were unpre-
dictable, grotesque. Yet when I wrote later about firing my
friend's magnum, I found myself describing not just the report of a magnum, but the feel of it in my hand—its potential,
its heft—and the shocking naturalness of it. Even though real
guns had not been allowed by my parents into our house, it
seemed, now, that during my whole boyhood I had unknow-
ingly been trained to relish and to find reassurance—even a
kind of phony confidence, a bravado—in the feel of a rifle
snugged up against the crook of my shoulder, or the feel of a
six-gun, making my right hand vital like a wand. For an American boy, aiming a toy rifle or wielding a toy six-gun (along
with all the fantasies they set off) is almost as fundamental as
swinging a baseball bat. The feel of a firearm in his hands
extends way beyond all rational considerations. It touches
upon his identity:

Some Basic Aesthetics

Out past the motels where town ends
and all the weather starts and the windy

grasses rattle their dried bracelets
Greg swung his pick-up off the county road
and we wobbled westward over ruts, looking
for some place safe to shoot.
What does being "American" feel like?
Steering the sights of his .357 magnum
from lucky rock to rock, I could feel
the solid handshake of its grip adjusting
me again in the comfortable old stance
that cap pistols set us in as boys.
Our trigger fingers light, whimsical,
we'd point, peremptory, directing
that hypothesis from to rock to darting
Indian to Kraut. This stance redoubled us
as in the batter's box, bats cocked.
Drop your guns. Keep your hands up. I expected
someday to own guns, to wear a tie.
Steering the magnum's trustworthy weight, sparing
a bush, sparing a dry patch, sparing a tree,
I parked my sights in front of a rock
where, on flatter ground, third base might be.
If it's possible to "feel" American
it was the first *Bam* boxing both my ears, numbing
half my face as, *Bam,* the limestone flared
a whiff of smoke, went out. *Bam.*
The valley harvested another crop of echoes
broadening into luxurious redundancy
upon redundancy. It was the thrill
of having your hands on so many cylinders
at once, all of them extra,
more capability than I would ever need.

American Male Honor

My last fistfight was with another eighth-grade boy named Steven Schutz, in right field, interrupting a game of "flies-and-grounders." Catch one fly ball or cleanly field three grounders, and you could trade places with the "batter" hitting fungos up into the nondescript grays of the New Jersey sky. It was an after-lunch recess in early April. There were around fifteen of us fanned out in a sort of hierarchy—the opportunistic little kids up front, eager to cut off grounders and to snag short pop-ups, older kids like me, with a more highly developed sense of honor, playing back waiting to estimate the long stately shots that would climb over the tree-line and come coasting in. As the ball climbed, if it was going to descend within your hegemony you'd "call" it—*I got it, I got it!*—then adjust your stride to it and lazily with an ease that was almost insolent nip it off one-handed in your webbing. But Schutz, a pudgy kid already over six feet tall at age thirteen, kept hogging flies destined for my territory.

I was small, frail, and physically deferential. With Texas leaguers that made it over the front ranks, just as I would start my timed lope forward Schutz would push in front of me—*I got it, I got it!*—and, with a lumbering intrepid greed that, I began to realize, was altogether characteristic of him, he would squeeze what should have been my fly ball. Schutz had done this for the third time in a row, and I was beginning to wonder if he had been bred properly, if Schutz had any of the normal, healthy sense of fairness—of common decency—that I had.

"American Male Honor" originally appeared in *TriQuarterly*, no. 73 (Fall 1988): 155–65, a publication of Northwestern University.

Schutz was a few strides directly to my right. *Tock!* Another routine fly appeared over the trees, and I prepared to receive it. I wouldn't even have to move. But Schutz was edging in front of me—*I got it, I got it!*—his huge buttocks were in my way. He had robbed me of my fly ball, robbed it practically from my glove. Almost speechless with indignation, I confronted him. I don't remember what I said. Somehow I had accidentally bumped my head against his intolerable shoulder, and with a sort of numb detachment I registered something unusual. My left fist had just passed across his jaw, and he was glaring at me, prim-lipped, his cherubic face a deep red. He was coming toward me. I was on the ground, and Mr. Snook, the eighth-grade teacher, was pleading—*Now boys! Boys! Break it up!*—as he attempted to pry Schutz off. I was relieved. It was confusing down there on the ground—not frightening, exactly, but confusing—and as I struggled shakily to my feet and went through the rapid, idiotic, rote handshake that Mr. Snook required of us, what little capacity I had for reason reminded me, with a parenthetical nudge, that I was lucky this time. I could have been hurt.

It is for honor that boys fight. It is in the name of honor that nations go to war. Honor is a deadly luxury. Honor originates as an aristocratic ideal, a traditional prerogative of gentility, from the code of the samurai to the chivalric ideal. Of course, in America, "luxury" is hardly what we think of as a genteel idea, it has been so thoroughly ruined by advertising and vulgarized by television. In America, "luxury," like sexual passion, like physical beauty, like any idea that could possibly be translated into material terms, has been converted into a marketable product. By watching television or going to the movies, we can buy as much "honor" as we want, in much the same way that, as Thorstein Veblen pointed out in 1899 in *The Theory of the Leisure Class,* American middle-class husbands lay claim to gentility: vicariously, by buying symbols of it, indulging in "conspicuous consumption."

The transformation of "honor" into a product seems harmless in itself—merely another silly "luxury," another of the adventitious pleasures of life in America. But honor, particularly male honor, is traditionally defined in terms of physical bravery, hence in terms of combat—human violence. More-over (as we tire of hearing, even though it's true), vicarious violence is marketed so pervasively on American media that it is, I think, next to impossible for an American boy not to dream wistfully about someday "punching out" somebody with a single, clean, cowboy haymaker. Certainly when slug-ging Steve Schutz with a left hook across the jaw—a stupid way to fight (if one must fight) because you can break the poor little bones in your hand—I was blindly copying all the comics and the movies that I had seen. I was adhering faith-fully to what I believed was the rule.

So deeply embedded in our culture, so constantly reiter-ated is the image of a good, clean fight in which a good guy teaches the bad guy a lesson, that if you're born a boy in Amer-ica, especially if you're physically small, you probably nurse all the way to your grave fantasies of proving your manhood by risking, and winning, such a fight. (All the clichés about "little-guy complexes" are true.) And when an actual fight develops before your eyes, along with the rest of the guys ringing the two combatants, you study the action with a rapt intensity that is a combination of voyeurism and terror. Here is the real thing—your darkest, dirtiest fantasy—being enacted. You can't help it: you wonder seriously if perhaps you ought to be in the middle of it, getting hurt instead of being on the side-lines. In a serious fistfight, the threshold between the specta-tors and the violence is infinitesimally fine. This is why fights in bars can so instantly become brawls. It doesn't take much booze to obliterate that remaining, fragile threshold. Besides, the Barroom Brawl is such a familiar event that, like the "hu-man wave" at a football game, it has acquired the status of a behavioral convention, indeed, of an institution. It is licenced. With all the other spectators, you're enfolded in a kind of velvet suspension, a cocoon of focused attention that, only when the fight's over and you find yourself shaking, emptied out, you realize must have been adrenaline, a kind of commu-nal adrenaline—the same kind of reaction that, I imagine, male dogs undergo by reflex when they meet and their hack-les go up.

Actual fights, though, by grown boys who have not been

trained to fight and who are not following a script, are shockingly ugly and inept. They are revolting. They remind me of when I once shot a squirrel out of a tree with a BB gun. It landed on its back, kicking, and, its legs flailing helplessly, gyrated and cartwheeled around on the lawn in a frenzy, out of its mind. It was in trauma. Finally it floundered into a hedge and disappeared. The last serious fistfight that I observed was equally epileptic. A bunch of us college students were waiting in the basement hall of the student union for the doors to the poolroom to be unlocked. It was almost 2:00 P.M.—a Saturday afternoon, in January, the college's final-examination period—and the small crowd was dispirited. There was a scuffling of activity. I looked up from my book. Were they opening the doors? No, it was Ernie Murphy. He was flailing as if trying to beat off a swarm of bees from his face, and right in front of him, his back to me, a boy with a greasy, black, DA haircut—a boy at least six inches shorter than Ernie (who was a good six feet two)—was slapping and flailing like mad as if trying to catch up with Murphy. In the silence, a faint, almost mechanical *smackety-smack* could be heard as they continued to swipe and slap madly, while the crowd, in mute deference, parted to give them room to fight just as, when someone is stricken in public and a crowd closes in to stare, the first cry that goes up is "Give him some air!" The two were in trauma. We had to give them air.

Smickety-smackety, the trauma worked its way along the hall, then collapsed, thrashing, and Ernie was on top, gasping "Nuff? *Nuff?*" A muffled reply, and Ernie let the boy up and sent him on his way with a brisk, friendly pat on the ass. The boy groped past us. He looked dazed, ancient, as if emerging from the hospital into daylight after major surgery, still half under the anaesthetic. His left eye was ruined. It was swollen closed, and under it bulged an exotic purple sac like a water balloon. The boy gingerly found his way outdoors, past a student coming in, who stared. "What happened?" A kid named Jimmy Silver, a slick, semi-hood who liked to hang out with tough guys but was careful never to get into a fight himself, spoke up in a cheerful voice: "Some kid was giving us some lip, so Ernie roughed him up a little." Silver winked. He was being coy, almost fey. He was spokesman for the gang. Ernie was their fist. The gang was his fist. Power is transitive. Silver was basking in it. He was thrilled, satiated. Vicariously.

I think of this—not of Murphy but of Silver—even now when watching news conferences on TV as different secretaries of defense, in their dark, conservative banker's suits, unroll some diagram like a grade-school social-studies map and, using a long pointer to indicate exactly where an enemy infection has attacked American forces, explain, in the same patient, pedantic voice that my grade-school teachers once used, the necessary surgical countermeasures that are being taken. The rhetoric is blood-curdling, because it *creates* reality. If Communism is a "cancer" that is spreading, then perhaps massive radiation treatments will one day be prescribed by the doctors in that world health organization known as the Pentagon.

It can be taken as a general rule of thumb, I think, that the rhetoric that "civilized" nations deploy to try to justify their military adventures becomes abstract and medical in direct proportion to the illegitimacy of those adventures. I was impressed by this a couple of years ago at the Topeka Air Show, where the U.S. Air Force Thunderbirds were featured. A professional announcer read from a script, and there was background music—the sound track from the movie *Chariots of Fire*. As the six F-15s took off, we were thrilled by what I can only think of as the Technological Sublime:

The History of the Wedge

In the brisk, pleasant voice of a surgeon
introducing his choice operation
the Air Force assured us how strictly
professional it is. *Armament,*
radius, objective: each word neutral
as a steel tool rinsed and drawn clean
from the Latin: a scalpel, a sterilized needle.
And we watched the latest knife:
five General Dynamics F-15's
like a five-card hand on the prowl

curve out over downtown Topeka and cut,
break east with a spurt, a sharp
black smudge and they're off on a new
vector, they are carving together,
that whole hand is rolling over
like one moving card revolving itself
to flash all five spades at once,
chased by the ragged mass of their roar,
the heavy furniture they trundle behind them
being hauled, torn over every rough floor
in the sky, rolling over roofs, ripping
and mending as the sixth svelte blade
clicks into formation, completing
that steadily traveling phalanx;
and there in the hazy autumn sky
we see this oldest formation of power,
abstract force focused in one ghostly
capital letter: Δ. The idea cruises
above us this afternoon, meeting
no resistance at all, circling
as if looking for victims. Nothing up there
to rape, but it can't stop moving,
it's coming back low, flat over the field
to shock it for kicks, the whole
history of the wedge is bursting
straight up the sky, trailing white crepe—
paper streamers in one, grand, Fourth-of-July
finale, fanfare proclaiming its victory,
Force flaunting itself, flexing
its engines, crowing, deafening us
with its form of laughter
as it lets its whole tool hang out
unsheathed, vertically, over 10,000 feet,
shaking it, shoving it in our faces.

I was thrilled by the jets, even thought they manifested
pure evil. How could evil be so beautiful? Or, put it another
way: Why did I find such charm in something of such evil?
There is only one possible answer, and it goes back to boyhood,

to the secret pleasure we take in vicarious violence—a pleasure that I think indicates how thoroughly and efficiently we have been indoctrinated by corporations into a kind of acquiesence to (even a kind of complicity with) the exercise of brute force in various (discreetly removed) areas of the world, as a means of controlling populations and ensuring sources of cheap labor to create that "standard of living" that we so take for granted. Violence originates as a political fact; but so insistently and artfully is it packaged on our media that we internalize it as a value: as boys we actually learn to *thrill* to it, to view it as something aesthetic. We never grow out of this. When I watch Caspar Weinberger on television gesture with his pointer to the latest map, I think of Jimmy Silver. I can sense, even on TV, the barely suppressed thrill that Weinberger gets from flashing his power in public, at deploying (however vicariously, however second- or third- or fourthhand) immeasurable deadly force. And as he clears his throat and begins using words like "deterrent" and "lesson," what I see on the TV screen is nothing so much as a sly, pious-sounding but utterly unscrupulous schoolboy posing as an adult—a boy who has learned that if you talk like a teacher, parody with a straight face the sanctimonious abstract rhetoric of grown-ups—you can get away with anything. What he means is this: This dirty foreign kid said something about our mother. I asked him: "What did you say about my mother?" He didn't answer, so I said, "Come on, step across this line, right *here*. I'm going to teach you not to talk like that. I'm going to teach you a lesson. Come *on*. I dare you, you little fairy. What's the matter? Are you chickenshit? Your mother's a slut. She fucks anything, and she *loves* it. Come on! I dare you! *Make my day*."

American foreign policy toward Communist countries has never developed above the level of boys in the schoolyard. It can't, because it is run by American men, and in America men are forever encouraged to go on entertaining their earliest boyhood fantasies about male honor. We're all like Huck Finn (and Huck's drunken, absent father): perhaps we need never graduate to real adulthood and to the boring restrictions of "sivilization." We can remain boys forever.

Twenty-five years after my fight with Schutz, as I commenced the study of *Shorin ryu* karate, I found that some vestigial gland in me still entertained the possibility that with sufficient technical preparation I could, without so much as being scuffed, administer an incredibly quick, magic volley of rude shocks to any of my enemies who might have been so naive as to have underestimated me. Before the formal pattern of each lesson, we would be introduced to a new "self-defense" technique. Each came with a scenario. *You're in a bar, and this guy grabs you in a bear-hug from behind.* Or: *You're in a bar, and this guy comes up to you head on, grabs your neck in both hands and starts to strangle you.* A few weeks into the class, I began to see that many of my classmates weren't studying karate for self-defense. When they went into a bar, they were hoping to meet this mythical "guy." My classmates could be divided into two categories. One type was like me. When somebody threw even a mock punch at them, their first and last impulse was to shrink from it, to cover up, to duck. The other type would risk being hit for the pleasure of hitting *you.* You could always tell who they were. As we'd shuffle and kick and block one-on-one like dance partners through each *ipon kumite,* or "one-point fight," they would study you with a neutral steadiness—almost a curiosity—their eyes expressionless as buttons. You were simply a target. Even though they'd stop their blows a literal hair breadth from your nose, from your kidney, from your temple, from your solar plexus, you could sense how much they'd love to follow through. It was embarrassing.

Karate classes are a little like square dances. With a partner you perform in rhythm coordinated routines, obeying a sort of "caller"—the *sensei*—who shouts out commands. You're being trained to react—to go for the throat with immediate accuracy—like a guard dog. Square dancing loses its appeal, though, when you're stuck with a partner who can't follow the caller, who gets "the grand right and left" mixed up. It's like trying to shake hands with somebody who has offered you their left hand. The timing is foiled. Some people have no talent for square dancing; I had no talent for karate. I was a lousy partner. I foiled everybody's timing. Our class was mostly white belts, a few yellow belts, a couple of orange belts. As we'd divide up into lines of partners, more and more frequently I'd find myself as if by accident with one of the milder, white-belted girls. Soon it became obvious that even *they* had more aptitude for fighting than I had. If the number of students in the class that day were an odd one, sometimes I would wind up with no partner at all. Like the "wallflower" at some high-school dance, I began to sympathize with the poor souls who, out of pity for me or out of their own carelessness, ended up being stuck with me for a partner.

The last karate class that I attended was visited by a local luminary from St. Louis, a black guy named Mel Brown, who was a fifth-degree (or was it a seventh-degree?) black belt. Brown was the single deadliest man I have ever met. His body was a pure weapon, but he, himself, was sultry, delicate, an aesthetician. *Shorin ryu* is a counterpunching style of karate, and much of it is developed out of a stance called *Nekoashi dachi:* the cat stance. And, in truth, Brown reminded one of a cat. Like a cat, he was a predator. But, like a cat, he kept this masked. He was discreet in the way a house cat is discreet. His discretion was sinister. He would never be deadly except intentionally, and then with absolute efficiency. As he fussed over my cat stance, touching me lightly now and then, posing me, he was so delicate that I was lulled into a sort of trance not unlike the passive complacency of Captain Delano as Babo shaves him, in Melville's *Benito Cereno.*

Brown began the class, as usual, by showing us a "self-defense" technique. As the Guy-in-the-Bar whaled his haymaker at you, you could slip inside it, blocking the punch and, grabbing the guy's hair or his ears with both hands, with a motion like that of snapping the lint out of a throw rug, you'd snap his head to give him whiplash. It seemed to typify all that we'd been learning, which was not how to knock Wrong out with a wholesome haymaker, but how, scientifically, to disable another human, piecemeal. Karate is a folk art. There is no possible means of dirty fighting we can think up that wasn't first thought up a thousand years ago by somebody else, and then refined through trial and error until it was perfect. Probably the instrument that affords us the most efficient mechanical advantage in flurries of close-in surgery is the elbow-strike: *empi zuki. Sieken zuki, mawasha seri, empi zuki:* the jargon of karate, like the Pentagon's surgical jargon, is sterile, technical, Platonic. The *katas* that we rehearsed until our arms and legs thrummed and ached were forms as abstract and ideal as Clausewitz's noumenal conceptions of war. I was especially attracted to a technique in which, by means of a front snap-kick propelling you forward into a side snap-kick that would half spin you toward your retreating opponent into position for *ura gera,* a back-kick, which would revolve you further toward him, facing him to begin the cycle of kicks again, you could literally dance your hapless adversary down the street in a continual hail of kicks without ever getting close enough to him that he could so much as scratch you. Of course, it was this last possibility that made the sequence so attractive to me—the idea that I might magically win Victory in a fight without having been in a fight at all.

Having finished demonstrating how to break somebody's neck, Mel Brown introduced us to a new *ipon kumite.* This one featured along with standard moves an exotic *uchi waza* in which, after a series of punches and blocks, you would combine hands and execute a double-handed strike to the face. My partner was a large, mild-mannered guy around my age, an orange belt. His name was Bob. The pattern of this *ipon kumite* was unusually elaborate, and Brown's commands were more abbreviated than what we were used to. I kept glancing sideways nervously, comparing my moves to those of my classmates. Had I lost my place? They all seemed to be perfectly synchronized, snapping their kicks and blocks like clockwork, sternly expressionless. Only *I* was lost. I felt sorry for my partner, who patiently went through the steps, hoping that I would be positioned correctly at each station in the drill. I placed my hands together for the new *uchi waza* and performed it. It felt awkward. I hoped fervently that this new *ipon kumite* would be over soon.

One of my knuckles had lightly ticked Bob's lip, and as I stepped back I was horrified to see that his lip was bleeding slightly. It meant that I was a disgrace, but at least the drill seemed finally to be over. As I rushed forward to apologize,

Bob was already assuring me with a quick shake of the head that it was nothing, it was okay: the totally honorable thing to do—acknowledge that it was an accident, and swallow, along with the discomfort, your annoyance. Nevertheless, I had hurt somebody who was not an enemy. As much as I had always secretly appreciated Honor, I was, apparently, incapable of it myself.

It was then, I think, that I first began to acknowledge that I was going to have to give up another unrealistic boyhood aspiration, like my fantasy of playing major-league baseball—just another of those losses that, grudgingly, you decide you'll accept as you become an adult, along with the loss of some more innocence. Finally, in America, albeit against their will and at an advanced age, boys will become adults. I began to understand the full extent to which my fantasy of winning a fistfight had not been pretty. It had been blind, part of an insidious, pervasive, and far-reaching ideology.

Boyhood Aesthetics

By the time I was nine, I knew by heart such beautiful information as the ground speed of the North American F-86F Sabre (683 mph at sea level), its combat radius (463 mi. with two 166.5 Imp. gal. tanks), its ferry range (1,525 mi.), and its armament (six .50 cal. machine guns). Even indoors, I could identify most commercial airliners by the tone of their engines, the most familiar being the unique and slightly gurgly song of the Douglas DC-3. The DC-4 and the DC-6, both four-engined planes, were distinguishable from the old Skytrain by the greater heft and authority of their engines, heard from greater altitude. The drone of the Lockheed Constellation was gruffer, choppier, more rugged, closer to noise than to music. The Boeing Stratocruiser was quiet, a discreet mutter. In my highly developed system of aesthetic priorities—a hierarchy in which four-engined planes were more beautiful than two-engined, and a three-engined plane was as freakish as a three-dollar bill—the Stratocruiser was particularly handsome. For one thing, it was more manly looking than most commercial airliners. Its wings and fuselage weren't rounded like those of the Douglas DC-series. A two-story liner, it was husky but not fat. It was ideally proportioned, the aeronautical equivalent of six feet four, 250 pounds. With its thin, severe wings clipped at the ends, its bottom view was reminiscent of the legendary B-29. It was a distant, fatherly plane, of great reserve, as dignified as the narrow neckties that became faddish later in the 1950s. Its value was high because it was rare. It would appear usually after supper, already at an impressive altitude, on a

From the *Iowa Review,* Winter 1981, 135–46.

northwest course, the late, orangish sun gilding its leading edges, making it all the more royal, more kingly. Through binoculars you could make out its red vertical stabilizer, the sumptuous red-and-blue markings of Northwest Airlines. To me, stranded there in the stagnant summer dusk, craning up at that magnificence still in daylight, the sun jeweling it like a brooch, it seemed as though the plane were already over Seattle and the Bering Strait was just beyond.

In my scale of values, private aircraft occupied the lowest rank and commercial the middle. The highest was restricted to warplanes, especially jets. This was in the early 1950s, when the only jets were military, and in my refined rating system, wing configuration had priority over number of engines: straight-wing lowest, sweptwing higher. Delta wing was off the scale, outside the sublunary sphere. Likewise, the faster a jet's ground speed, the higher its value. At around 700 mph a plane began to blur into myth. As for the sound barrier—it was simply the limit of the literal. *Supersonic* meant *transcendental.*

One of the great misfortunes of my life, I believed, was that where we lived, near the Great Swamp in northern New Jersey, was far from any air force base. Jets were all the more beautiful for their rarity, and the instant I heard one I'd go pounding outdoors with binoculars and scour the sky. Usually the tiny moving center that I sought was too high up in the bright haze to be discerned, or it was above the clouds. If it were a clear day, I'd look for the moving chalk-streak of a vapor trail boring through the blue after the pale germ that kept outrunning it. But unless it were a big plane, a bomber, even through field glasses all you could tell was whether the jet was straight-wing or swept-back. At that height, lit was a stratospheric glow, the jets seemed to acquire a ghostly quality. Any swept-back jet might have been some new, top-secret experimental prototype on its way west to Edwards Air Force Base.

Even now, I can't wholly understand why it was so important to make positive identification. Somehow, unless a jet could be named, it remained elusive. I couldn't possess even the memory of it securely enough. When, in the rare instances that a jet would appear over our house low enough that I had a chance to recognize it, I felt so lucky that it seemed literally a form of grace. I can remember early in my airplane religion one sultry Saturday morning in spring hearing a strange and mighty drone undercut by bass poundings so deep that the house, even the earth, seemed to pulsate, and rushing outside to see the sky literally blanketed with formations of B-36s, herds of them all shoulder to shoulder laboring west, their progress immeasurably slow. The planes were high, glowing, silvery silhouettes occasionally spewing the wisp of a contrail. Finally, after what seemed half an hour, the last of these formations labored below the trees, and the morning was silent, diminished as if abandoned by its gods. Where were those great, saurian planes headed? I don't know. But looking back on that morning, on those tremendous, slow (435 mph) muscle-bound heavy bombers, I wonder if, like a herd of brontosauruses; they weren't making their last migration west toward extinction in some desert dump-site.

❧

Not to dwell anywhere near an air force base was to be isolated wretchedly in the boondocks, in a place without culture. It seemed as serious a deprivation as life without one of the new television sets the Thompsons had bought. Mrs. Thompson had graciously consented to let my brother and me watch *The Howdy Doody Show* each weekday evening on their massive Admiral with its shimmery 8-inch screen. When, each night at dusk, satisfied, brimming with the shocking news of Mr. Bluster's latest plot, we'd lope home across Thompsons' field, entering our silent house where Alan and Jaynet sat expressionless in the living room frowning into *Harper's* and *The New Yorker* was like returning to the dark ages.

Everybody, or so it seemed, had been blessed but me. Uncle David and Aunt Peggy, up in South Hadley, Massachusetts, actually found the jet traffic from Westover Field a nuisance. When I asked my cousin Larry what kind of fighters they had up there, he remarked wryly that he didn't know, but there sure were a lot of them.

Jaynet's brother, Uncle Lin, and his family were even luckier. They lived no more than five miles from Wright-Patterson

Field, in Ohio. One day I discovered that, in our Hammond's atlas, the maps of the individual states showed the names and locations of air force bases: Biggs, Stewart (quite near, a possibility!), Moses Lake, Nellis, and, of course, Edwards, the equivalent in my religion to the Vatican.

I spent long, productive afternoons going over these maps state by state until I was satisfied that I'd memorized the names and locations of every air force base in America. The most unpromising and nondescript area in the country, such as Texas, could suddenly become interesting. Nearly every state had at least one shrine, its cultural center that I resolved to visit if I were ever in the area. Even lowly New Jersey had some culture—McGuire Air Force Base, a two-hour drive south, in Wrightstown, by Fort Dix. One day, during the gray lull of a spring vacation, Jaynet suggested brightly that we spend a day in Wrightstown "looking at the jets."

It was one of the best days of my life. Some parts of New Jersey are so glum, so blighted that all the worst elements of the landscape exhibit, like a Charles Sheeler painting of heavy industry, a somber aesthetic consistency, a grisly beauty. The view from the Pulaski Skyway over the Jersey Meadows is like that: the sickly waters of the Hackensack and Passaic, rotten pilings, the tarnished innards of the chemical industry arrayed like organ pipes below—an infernal orchestra—the blackened brick faces of tenements, the bridges measuring the depths of the smoky atmosphere south—the Bayonne Bridge, the Goethals Bridge, the Verrazano Narrows Bridge—the hazy smiles of the bridges arching over the gray waters like arias. It is this difficult beauty that was William Carlos Williams's obsession:

> There is a plume
> of fleshpale
> smoke upon the blue
>
> sky. The silver
> rings that
> strap the yellow

brick stack at
wide intervals shine
in this amber

light—not
of the sun not of
the pale sun but

his born brother
the declining season.

As a boy I understood this kind of beauty. It was like the dubious beauty of a maximum-security facility, and air force bases had it—miles of storm fence, barbed wire, hangars, towers, searchlights, the runways like superhighways running off to the horizon where vague events occurred out in the oily distance, and the silvery mirages of the jets congregated.

For about four hours, parked on the cinders of the shoulder, armed with a picnic lunch of chicken salad sandwiches, Jaynet and I watched squadrons of North American F-86D Sabres maneuver. Some of them, as they lagged in low over the barracks, their engines peeping like teakettles leaking a sooty smudge of fumes, whispered by so close that I could see all the networks of pop-rivets on the fuselage, the nub of the pilot's helmet as the huge machine sank away sighing over the fence down into the zone where I could not trespass.

≥♣

In time, I was to visit other shrines. I would spend, with Alan, one sallow, hazy afternoon at the perimeter of Otis Air Force Base, in Cape Cod, until I was surfeited on the shape of the F-94C Starfire—a shape I'd memorized from the three-view drawings in Green and Pollinger's *Observer's Book of Aircraft* but that, until that morning, I had never hoped to see.

I would spend most of a day with Uncle Lin, on a bus tour of Wright-Patterson Field, a day climaxed by a virtual banquet of different jets parked by a hangar, a gourmet sampling that included a dark, mantislike, twin-engined jet that I realized must be an actual Martin B-57, in its night camouflage. It had an aura of evil, like the model of the sinister, twin-boomed Northrop P-61 Black Widow all-weather night-fighter that Tony Remsen and I had made. The Black Widow! Fully assembled, with all its aerials and guns like the feelers and stingers of a fat, black scorpion, it literally bristled with harm.

By then, like any member of the Audubon Society, I was keeping a list of all the commercial and military planes of which I'd made "positive identification." If I'd been a few years older, I would have joined the Ground Observer Corps, a civilian volunteer organization that, like the term *civil defense,* now sounds prehistoric: the mission of the Corps was to identify Russian bombers that had slipped through U.S. radar. I kept my list in my desk, rubber-banded to the heavy wad of two hundred "Friend-or-Foe" airplane cards I'd collected by buying sheets of brittle, flesh-colored bubble gum that I'd immediately discard. I had the only complete set on Pleasantville Road, the result of dogged barter.

But the list was much more valuable than the cards. True, great beauty was prefigured by the cards—the beauty of the Gloucester Javelin, a British delta wing jet, its speed "secret" but "estimated at over 700 mph"—a vampire-shaped jet that, like the British Vickers delta wing bombers, in sunlight was less a gothic phantasm than a silver sprite descended directly from the realm of faerie.

Early in my tenderness for planes, I'd noticed that, even going so far back as World War II, the shapes of British planes were more organic than those of American planes. Compared to the stubby, square-tipped wings of the P-51 Mustang, the wings of the Supermarine Spitfire and its cousin, the Hawker Hurricane, were curved like vowels more fully rounded, as if the very shapes of the planes had a British accent. The gray, pug-nosed P-51 with its blocky shoulders was clearly a tough guy, a city kid. The Spitfire, with its wings like curved leaves and its canopy set jauntily far back on the fuselage like the cockpit of a baby Austin, seemed streamlined for the sake of beauty alone, a thoroughbred. With its sand-and-spinach markings, it was pastoral, aristocratic, refined. The P-51 was a machine: the Spitfire was a gull.

In aircraft design, each country had a dialect. The most

fascinating because it was so shadowy was, of course, that of the enemy. Every spring, as impatiently as the CIA, I awaited May Day, when the Russians might reveal some new jets—jets that, in the airplane books I was now collecting, were always depicted by grainy, amateurish, black-and-white snapshots taken, I knew, by our spies. MIGs! The expletive was a synonym for knee-jerk evil—Apaches bursting out of ambush, riding down out of the sun. The MIG-15 was easy to recognize: like the Sabre but with an obscenely high tail-fin. And, like the shark, like any stylized enemy, all MIGs were bleakly identical, devoid of humor. They were beautiful; but like the beauty of the Empire's stubby functional craft in *Star Wars,* theirs was of a minimalist sort. The MIG-15 resembled the faceless, wooden, suicidally obedient, brainwashed Communists who, according to Mrs. Lee, my fourth-grade teacher, piloted them. Puritan, gray, crude—the stylistic equivalent to the "burp gun" I studied in such war comics as *Two-Fisted Tales*—the MIG was issued in gray carbon copies from a world where, it seemed obvious, conditions were too arid for romance.

Whereas the MIG possessed so little individuality that it didn't even have a name, our planes were human. Reciting the lineage of the Boeing bomber series, with its progressively elaborated motif—*Flying Fortress* to *Super Fortress* to *Stratojet* to *Stratofortress*—I never doubted that the men who designed these planes and named them were like me, moved by the same longings: the men at Lockheed who dreamed up the *Shooting Star,* then the *Starfire,* then the *Starfighter;* the men at Republic who dreamed first the *Thunderjet,* then the *Thunderstreak,* the *Thunderflash,* and finally the F-103 *Thunderchief.*

❧

My list of planes I'd spotted was more than a list of shapes. It was a list of complex and elusive experiences, just as baseball statistics were, for me then, not so much a measure of performance or efficiency as an aesthetic measurement from which you could magically evoke the peculiar mystique—the character—of a star. *Batting Average: .344. Stolen Bases: 29. RBI: 63. HR: 4. Hits: 221*—these numbers *were* Richie Ashburn in his 1951 season for the Phillies. *Won: 19. Lost: 11. ERA: 3.30.*

This is the essence of the Dodgers' Preacher Roe in 1950. Likewise, certain shapes—the three-view silhouettes of planes—that I used to whet my imagination were the shorthand to flashes of irrecoverable beauty.

A couple of weeks after coming home from Ohio (on a Martin 404), I untwisted the elastic band, unfolded my list, and erased the B-57. You just couldn't take credit for spotting a plane on the ground. The parked, placid B-57 was like a stuffed scarlet tanager I'd seen in the Museum of Natural History, oddly listless. It was too available. The natural habitat of planes was sky: Steep, windy April skies when, in the narrow blue chasms between the fraying walls of stratocumulus, if you were lucky, you could glimpse the mica fleck of a little fighter leaping the gap, catch the lonely echo it left crumbling down the sky-canyon like shreds of shale debris. Hazy afternoon skies, stained orange, through which you could hear the growl of a Lockheed Constellation heading west but couldn't locate it until it was almost behind Cissels' spruce trees, when the sun hit it right, and the Constellation, kindling like a tiny candelabra in the general glare, lived up to its name. Solid slate skies when sounds carried for miles, and the thin howl of a jet was like the rumor of some great trouble above the clouds. The three-view drawing of the navy's Douglas Skyknight was my shorthand not just for the experience of seeing it. It was part and parcel of the weather, of the light, of the whole day which had been its habitat.

The day I saw two Skyknights was one of those rare days when, to escape the stifling summer heat, my parents had decided we'd go to the shore. The announcement the night before filled me with quiet determination. Never had we gone to the shore when I hadn't spotted several warplanes—blue navy planes with white insignias. Even commercial planes like the banal DC-3 acquired new value in military dress, if only because they prefigured the possibility of tougher, faster aircraft. Although I shunned church and was pretty sure I didn't believe in God, the night before we left for the shore I was careful to pray. I asked God to make sure a few jets were around. Then, in case God wondered why I was always asking him for things and never giving him anything back, I quickly thanked him for all the things I knew I should be grateful for, though I couldn't remember exactly what they were at the moment. Finally satisfied that I'd done all I could, I closed my eyes, stretched out on top of the sheets and waited for the fan to lull me to sleep.

The fifty-mile drive south to Sea Bright, in the days before turnpikes, was dull and slow and ugly. But for me it was thrilling. For one thing, our route crossed two major railways, the B&O in Plainfield and the Pennsylvania in Metuchen. In those days, trains had for me something of the glamor of planes, especially streamlined passenger trains. To behold one of these—say, the *Royal Blue* on its way to Washington—its chrome coach cars basking on the dingy, soot-blackened concrete overpass in the center of Plainfield, left me feeling as if a queen who was both beautiful and good, from a realm that I was positive had to exist, had deigned, in her silk regalia, to light up the drabness of Plainfield with a promise of some gleaming, streamlined, frictionless future I might someday be ready for.

Farther south, if the sky were clear, were glimpses of the Manhattan skyline. Stephen and I had memorized the names and shapes of New York's skyscrapers, the way you memorize the names of mountain peaks in order to recognize their countenances. The Empire State Building, the Chrysler Building, the RCA Building—they were like a family standing together in midtown, king, queen, and prince. As if the Empire State Building were a movie star, we both agreed that the thin view of him was handsomest. South of Perth Amboy, chugging along in our 1949 Plymouth Suburban, the Manhattan skyline was a cluster of spires so tiny and dim that, like the streak of a high jet, it was all the more tantalizing. On the rare instances when it was clear enough to see it, Stephen and I would get excited. It was as if, out of the characterless huddle of the New Jersey landscape, the faint suggestion of a beautiful and familiar face in profile had appeared on the horizon.

Then there were the bridges—gray, lacy, each with its serious expression, like people we knew out there over the choppy water of Raritan Bay—the serious bridges, old acquaintances we could visit only a few times a year. I'll never understand why it is that, as kids, we attach this charge of emotional energy to things. We did it with marbles. *King, Big Bubber*—each possessed a personality and an aesthetic ranking. But I think that, even as adults, our apprehension of beauty must always involve some sense of subjective recognition.

Shortly before noon, while the sand was still cool, I glanced up from a wet deviled egg that was like an eyeball I was trying to keep sand out of as I separated it from its waxed paper. My sixth sense for jets had picked up, over the wash of a sadly listless surf, the indolent whistle jets make as they coast. And there they were, two chunky Skyknights maybe a thousand feet up, out over the water, in no hurry, sauntering north toward Sandy Hook. There was no question what they were. And as the twin specks grew finally indistinguishable from the grains of light and haze to the north somewhere over New York Bay, and I gave the south a cursory surveillance to make sure no more miracles were about to fly out of it, I felt as though a couple of movie stars, Roy Rogers and Gene Autry, had come past and only I had noticed them. I knew that all the hours I spent daydreaming about planes and drawing them had paid off, that it was my devotion, my faith that had enabled the two stalwart Skyknights to manifest themselves out of the hot dreariness of summer vacation.

ह∾

Beauty—our subjective sense of it, our conviction that we're beholding it—involves, as I've already hinted, a feeling that is similar but not identical to the feeling we experience when we recognize something familiar—a face, a car, a landscape. Like a three-year-old lost in a crowded supermarket who picks out its mother's face, we discover that we have memorized the unique character—the singular gestalt—of some part of our experience. But the three-year-old's feeling upon glimpsing Mommy—a flood of relief and, perhaps, rage at her for disappearing—isn't aesthetic. For an experience to be aesthetic, it must involve some degree of abstraction. In order that something seem beautiful, we must discover in it some sense of its typicality; for recognition of the beautiful involves a paradox of feelings: a sense of its singularity and typicality

both. To me, as a boy, the beauty of the Douglas Skyknight—
of the three-view drawing or the actual plane in the air—
combined both feelings. Like any familiar face, the Skyknight
possessed a unique shape. To identify this shape—to name
it—was to attribute to it typicality.

The subtler the set of cues by which we recognize something, and the greater the degree of abstraction involved
when we match these cues to some abstract pattern, the more
aesthetic our feeling is. The lost three-year-old who finds his
mother senses her familiarity but not her typicality. This imbal-
ance between uniqueness and typicality defines the lower limit
of the range of aesthetic experience. The upper limit is ex-
ceeded by people who too readily reduce a potentially aesthetic experience into an abstraction, who ignore its uniqueness, its quality, and dwell entirely on its typicality. The notion
that Robert Frost's "Stopping by Woods on a Snowy Evening"
is a poem "about the Freudian death-wish" is an upper-limit
violation. Within these limits lies the range of experience that
I'll call "aesthetic" and that I would describe thus: the subjective sense of beauty is an intimation of the elusive character of
experience. We all know that gray suspense of a cold, late-
November afternoon, when snow is imminent. Our intimation, "It's going to snow," is aesthetic. When William Stafford
writes, "a land that / began to tense itself all day for deliberate
snow," we know what he means. And we know exactly what
Richard Hugo means in "Duwamish" when he writes, "Gray /
cold like the river. Cold like 4 P.M. / on Sunday."

There is another aspect to aesthetic experience that perhaps
should go without saying. Aesthetic experience is restricted to
experience in which we find value. This excludes, by definition, those domains of experience that we associate with shame.
It also excludes experience too easily available. For me, as a boy,
the deepest aesthetic contemplation entailed trying to summon
from a three-view drawing the way the shabby sunlight
brushed and slid off the wingtip tanks of the Starfires as, buoy-
ant in the heat-shimmer, they'd bank way out over the scrub
and macadam flats of Otis. It meant trying to describe in my
mind's eye the pure trajectories they traced as curve after curve
dissolved in the drab afternoon like caresses that never last

quite long enough to grasp. It was to squint through field glasses at a tiny, pale arrowhead plunging through a snowy brow of cumulus, working against time to try to match the moment against pages of shapes, to find its name.

ঌ

The impulse to name something is the impulse to "collect" it in the sense of incorporating it into a familiar context, usually that of a list. This list may be of minerals, stuffed birds, or artists' canvases. It may be simply a list of words, a vocabulary. But the instinct to "collect," in the figurative sense in which I use the term here, is also aesthetic. In listing the planes I'd glimpsed, I was trying to collect a special type of experience. What I was after was not a literal collection of planes. Had my parents bought me for Christmas a surplus F-80 Shooting Star and trucked it into the backyard, it would, like the B-57 that I erased from my list, have been far less valuable to me than the apparition of those twin Skyknights over Sea Bright. Literal collection didn't satisfy me. That was the lazy and ultimately unsatisfying alternative to art.

The theme of collection as a perversion of the aesthetic impulse is a familiar one in literature. Probably the most famous poem on the theme is Browning's "My Last Duchess." In the most explicit way, that poem presents the notion that art, epitomized by the painting that the duke has commissioned of his wife before murdering her, is the best available means to possess (to the limited extent that is possible) the most elusive beauty. At the same time, the poem demonstrates in the crudest way that to own and possess something beautiful, you have to kill it.

The theme of collection as evil abounds in fiction, too. For example, both Gilbert Osmond of Henry James's *Portrait of a Lady* and Edward Casaubon of *Middlemarch* are collectors whose mania for collection is life-destroying. Osmond, who collects art objects, has transformed his daughter, Pansy, into a sad, perfectly mannered doll. Once Isabel Archer is in his possession, through marriage, he loses interest in her. The scholar, Casaubon, who possesses, also through marriage, the young, beautiful, and serious Dorothea Brooke, maintains her as a peripheral ornament to his life while he busies himself with his life's work, which is, appropriately enough, to compile a "key to all mythologies." Probably the most grueling treatment of this theme in prose fiction is John Fowles's *The Collector*, in which a psychopathic young man, by means of chloroform, kidnaps a beautiful, young art student and attempts to keep her as one keeps a pet or a live butterfly in a glass case. In all of these works, we see that to treat the beautiful as part of a tangible collection is to deny its life. Indeed, to freeze movement is to deny the nature of life itself, as illustrated vividly by the following poem by Albert Goldbarth:

The Origin of Porno
1878: the Muybridge equine series

Studying the horse, we understand
how hard-core followed the invention
of photography. There's a dark compelling
muscle framed by the flanks. There's

a question, an academic question, of at
which point in a leap the female breast
is highest? In the early stopwatched studies,
light slopes down the breasts like a scree. There's

a question of time, there's a sepia
exactitude. The powder erupts:
in the foreground—two lovers/ a basket/ red wine.
In the back, a clocked thoroughbred sudses.

Is there ever a moment when all four feet
leave the ground? And so we invent pornography.

It wasn't until the late 1960s, when I was living in San Francisco, that I was actually granted my boyhood dream—proximity of a military air base. Our flat, situated on the hills above Castro Street, faced east directly at Alameda Naval Air Station ten miles across the bay. Late afternoons were best for observing Alameda, when the light would be at my back, and the white buildings assumed a frozen brilliance as they stared blindly at the sun, a hillside of white rubble, and the hard blue strip of the East Bay looked as if you could step across it.

Through field glasses you could see the day's training flights straggling in, slow insects floating diagonally down across the powder blue profile of the hills where, as the sun set, a picture window twenty miles away might echo the sun so that even without field glasses it was as if in the mountains behind Oakland there had lodged a reddish white star. Most of the jets were Douglas Skyhawks—they resembled bats more than hawks—and McDonnell Phantoms, mean-looking attack planes with wasplike bodies and stubby, meat-cleaver wings, all business. Sometimes during the day a Phantom would curve back across the bay and over the rooftops, maybe a thousand feet up. It had a characteristic sound, like heavy canvas being ripped. Commercial jets merely roar: military jets snarl.

Once, for a couple of weeks, a carrier like a long, gray cloud—the only reminder that there was a war going on in Asia—existed out in that silent blue shimmer. On the deck were lined up copies of a snub-nosed jet I couldn't quite identify. They might have been Chance-Vought Corsairs. It no longer mattered very much. As in this recollection, planes, by then, were little more than emblems. It was no longer some elusive shape in the clouds that I wanted to name, but the broader character of my experience—a dim countenance that, singular as it is, may also typify the devious, unlikely ways that a boy, growing up in a country like America—a country in which military hardware is so much a part of the landscape that we no longer notice it—may have to take to satisfy the human hunger for beauty, scrounging for it in even the grimmest facts that we have come to live with, in the perfection of our weapons.

II

American Anaesthetics

Imaginary Fathers

In July 1985, about two months before he died, I had my last serious conversation with my father. It was a short conversation, and it was not good. In one blow, it seemed to cancel all the gains I thought I had made in a lifetime of trying to win his attention and respect.

Alan was eighty-one. He had, from a lifetime of smoking Pall Malls, been suffering severely from emphysema, and during my visit he could sometimes be found seated before the backyard picnic table, motionless, his head bowed, as if in profound contemplation. Cupped in his hands like an offering was a silk handkerchief.

Was he praying? Never. His philosophy was "logical positivism." The equivalent to Jesus, for Alan, was Bertrand Russell. In fact, Alan cultivated, rather obnoxiously, I thought, some of Bertrand Russell's mannerisms: a certain stubborn scowl when he was about to pronounce upon a matter of principle. One of his favorite conversations—a kind of set piece, delivered in donnish tones—was a lecture disproving the existence of God.

After a stint at the Cavendish laboratory in Cambridge, England, Alan had acquired a faintly British accent that he would accentuate in certain rhetorical situations, when he might pronounce the word *structure* as "*struck*-chuh." With furled, thunderous brow: "Mathematics is the study of *struck*-chuh!" Alan was built like Russell, too—short, wiry, small-boned. He wasn't thin enough to be called "elfin." He was more like a gnome—a small gnome. Bent over his silk handkerchief in the backyard,

From *Creative Nonfiction*, no. 4.

Alan wouldn't be praying. He'd be drooling. For spans of twenty or thirty minutes, he'd remain immobilized, captive to the flow of mucus from his nose.

But he was indoors, now, at the kitchen table, and we were talking about one of Bertand Russell's chosen—Ludwig Wittgenstein.

I mentioned that I'd always regretted not having learned German, that German still seemed to be the language of the marketplace in Europe.

Alan allowed that it *was* regrettable, and then added this pronouncement: "Son, until you know German, you'll never understand Western Culture."

"Until you've played shortstop," I retorted coldly, "you'll never understand *American* culture," and Alan realized that he'd stung me. He immediately shut up.

But the exchange seemed to epitomize all of the differences between us, especially the pain inherent in being, though reasonably smart, intellectually inferior to one's father. Why the hell did he have to rub it in?

ਕ

Alan had never deigned to do ordinary things with me; for he'd never thought of himself as ordinary, nor had he ever much cared to be. In fact, he was *not* ordinary. A child prodigy—a polymath with not only a photographic memory, but a pronounced musical talent, and a poetic imagination— Alan should have been born in England into an aristocratic elite, like Bertrand Russell or the mathematician G. H. Hardy. They would have cultivated him like some kind of rare orchid, as somebody special, for that is how he regarded himself. My Aunt Eth recalls that when he returned from his first semester at Harvard he announced that from now on he refused to sleep on anything but "black satin sheets." He was conspicuously, proudly eccentric. In high school in Montclair, New Jersey, he was teased mercilessly. He once described to me how the students would line up behind him and mimic his bouncing gait when he walked. Born in 1904, the same year as the physicist J. Robert Oppenheimer, his torments recall

Oppenheimer's, as described by Richard Rhodes, in *The Making of the Atomic Bomb:*

> When he was fourteen, to get him out of doors and perhaps to help him find friends, his parents sent him to camp. . . . He was shy, awkward, unbearably precious and condescending and he did not fight back. . . .When the camp director cracked down on dirty jokes, the other boys, the ones who called Robert "Cutie," traced the censorship to him and hauled him off to the camp icehouse, stripped him bare, beat him up—"tortured him," his friend says—painted his genitals and buttocks green and locked him away for the night. Responsibly he held out to the end of camp but never went back. . . . Very quickly everybody admitted that he was different from all the others and very superior.

But there was a crucial difference between Alan, on the one hand, and Oppenheimer. After graduating from Harvard, instead of going straight to graduate school and a doctorate, Alan had left academic life in order to work as an accountant in New York City. His mother was dying of tuberculosis. Forever after, as a scientist, in spite of his intellect, Alan was playing catch-up ball.

Later in his life, when Alan had on the basis of his bestselling book *Crystals and Crystal Growing* acquired a national reputation as an educator and won the Millikan Award of the American Association of Physics Teachers, whenever other physicists invited him to join their departments, they discovered, to their astonishment, that he lacked the Ph.D. All negotiations would stop. He could never be hired full-time by a university physics department. He would remain at the Bell Telephone Laboratories until retirement.

I remember when, wondering aloud whether I should go for a Ph.D. in English, Alan actually tried to discourage me from it.

"Nope. You don't need one."

I didn't believe him.

ॐ

As somebody special: that was how Alan tried to lead his life. In a way, he was as romantic as Don Quixote. He would construct his own version of the Bloomsbury Circle in the suburbs of New Jersey. It was almost possible. Nothing I've read describes the feel of the household that Alan and Jaynet ran more closely than Virginia Woolf's description of the Ramsay household in her novel *To the Lighthouse.* The scientists whom Alan collected around himself and who were regularly in and out of our house were some of the most intellectually successful men in the world. They included two Nobel laureates in physics, Philip Anderson and William Shockley, men like Philip Morrison, who'd been involved in the Manhattan project, as well as men in other fields, like the composer Virgil Thomson. Alan had assembled a sort of salon. But as fathers, they were inept. They were like spoiled children, far too self-centered to love their own kids.

Alan, himself, had never particularly wanted to be bothered with raising children. "Interesting little organisms," he was fond of joking. Like the Ramsay household, indeed like the households of most of the other Bell labs scientists, ours was cemented by the tireless, almost heroic ministrations of a mother whose loyalty to her husband and determination to spare him the boring details of daily life was self-abnegating. From the sexually "liberated" perspective of today, my parents' nearly fifty-year-long marriage looks quaint, almost comic. Jaynet even bought Alan's clothes for him as for a child: she would pick them out and present them to him. Years later, when reading in Swift's *Gulliver's Travels* "The Voyage to Laputa," a satire of the intellectuals in the Royal Academy who live on a floating island and are so absorbed in their study of the music of the spheres that the only way to get their attention is through a "flapper," I realized at once that the "flappers" were the scientists' wives.

Weekends, our household tiptoed carefully around the dining room, where Alan had barricaded himself to write. I remember being dispatched to call him to lunch, one Sunday, and marveling at the legal pad he was writing on. Page after page of mathematical nomenclature, algebra. It had been jotted in a breakneck, accurate script, like the tracks of an Olympic skier cutting and banking downhill through a succession of gates, digging in with a parenthesis, then a series of linked quadratics closed off with another slice of a parenthesis, and so on down into another concatenation. It was as if Alan's mind had been continuously outrunning the hand that could record its movement. It was Mind on its feet made visible. In 1985, when Alan died and I was clearing out the house, I came across all those legal pads covered with identities. I discovered what he had been up to. He had been trying to prove Fermat's Last Theorem.

❧

We lived in the country on seven acres in an old farmhouse my parents had bought in the Depression for five thousand dollars and had restored. It was a place of long silences, creaking floors. Its interior felt like a judge's chambers, different shades of amber brought to a high Augustan polish. It was a simple house, without ornament, its tidyness and simplicity dictated by a Puritan aesthetic that I associate with a political liberalism whose style, for all its apparent modesty, asserts a kind of moral arrogance. It's the arrogance implicit in the Socratic dictum, "The unexamined life is not worth living." In other words: "If you have not examined your life with the rigor that *we* have, then your life isn't worth living."

Every once in a while, auspiciously, a car would go crackling past on the gravel road. It was an event. On weekends, there was nothing to do. I liked baseball, but there was hardly anyone to play catch with. I spent entire weekends alone hitting a threadbare tennis ball out into the field east of our house and judging the result: a low liner for a single. A higher liner that ricocheted off the pear tree for a double, a triple if it hit high up and took an erratic bounce into "the corner." A homer if it carried over Thompsons' hedge. A double play if I hit a pop-up and could catch my own pop fly with one hand.

One late-April Sunday when I was twelve and conspicuously bored, Jaynet *ordered* Alan out of the dining room to play catch with me. It was around two-thirty on a pale afternoon, maybe an hour to go before the return of a hopelessness as faithful as the tide, the growing certainty that tomorrow was Monday: school. I remember that afternoon vividly. It was the one and only time that Alan played catch with me. And it was embarrassing.

Out on the grizzled lawn, where a couple of daffodils had declared themselves, in the weak New Jersey light, Alan resembled nothing so much as a small animal surprised outside its burrow. The sunlight puzzled him. Gamely he held out my Uncle Matt's old catcher's mitt as a target for me to hit. I had a good arm. I thought that quite possibly I could blow his hand off. I tried to. The throw was wild. He lurched sideways, knocked the ball down. Stiffly, in a dignified manner, he stooped, scooped the ball up. He was still expressionless. With an abrupt push, as if he were fending off a bee, he forced it back.

We went through this ritual for twenty minutes. Then I let him go. It was costing him too much. He didn't know how to do this. He had no idea what to say, like "nice throw" or "a little high." He was completing, doggedly and without pleasure, an assignment.

By the time I was sixteen and playing some organized baseball, I had resolved that, when I had a son, I would play with him as often as I could. I would give him the very kinds of attention that Alan had, either out of debility or plain self-centeredness, refused me. It was not an idle fantasy. It was a silently resolved strategy. My desire, of course, was as sentimental as it was psychological—the ideal dad would take his boy fishing, I thought, though now I know better.

≥▲

"Strategy." I think that the strategic manner in which I imagined nurturing a son I leaned from Alan, though his strategic bent of mind was never turned to nurturance. When Alan would level his attention on a project, however, the intensity of his concentration was almost terrifying. It was absolute. And that is primarily the way I remember him: watching him at work. Other fathers might cuss out a lawnmower that wouldn't catch. Or kick the car. Alan would simply stop. He'd stop and think awhile, his breath wheezing through his nose—hiss and hiss like something mechanical until, abruptly, a solution clicked. Then, step by step, arranging parts in the sequence they'd come loose, he'd direct at the poor lawn-mower a logic even that sullen machine could not refute. Then, just as systematically, he'd refit each wrench upon its Peg-Board silhouette, re-index every drill bit, every nail—this small, half-German intellectual who, I came to believe, could probably figure anything out if he decided to put his mind to it. Stephen and I were never sure just what he thought of us. Had he hated us, he wouldn't have shown it. When, in a reasoning, mildly troubled tone he once explained to me, *In war, people hurt with tools*, it gave me the creeps. He was one of the men inventing those same tools. He was a patient man. There was no telling what he might invent.

During World War II, when the Bell labs was doing weapons research, Alan developed a crystal useful in the sonar detection of submarines. In the late 1950s, when Soviet Russia stunned America by being the first nation in the world to put a satellite in orbit, there was a scramble in this country to upgrade curricula in science and mathematics. Nuclear and thermonuclear weapons had, by that time, been perfected anyhow; so many of America's top physicists turned their talents toward pedagogy.

Alan's book for the Doubleday Science Series, *Crystals and Crystal Growing*, was like a cookbook. The almost apparitional way in which a crystal could reveal itself inside a solution was tantalizing, mysterious. Most crystals are beautiful, and like botanical phenomena they appeal to the human instinct for classification. Crystallographic taxonomies are geometrical, and in the early 1960s, Alan began constructing, with cardboard and Elmer's Glue, three-dimensional, polyhedral models. He worked at home a lot. He'd stump down cellar at nine and, troll-like, come stumping back upstairs for a Manhattan cocktail at five. He worked on weekends.

By 1985, the polyhedra had almost entirely taken over the house. The geometrical structures that filled Alan's head were irrepressible. They had broken out into the light of common day and lived, like placid pets, beside us, grazing on counters and bookshelves. Or they hung from the ceiling, human spider webs, ideal solar systems, Mind made visible.

Betty Wood, Alan's colleague at the lab and, like him, a crystallographer, told me once that the character Felix Hoenikker in Kurt Vonnegut's novel *Cat's Cradle* was based, in part, on Alan. It's possible. In Vonnegut's 1969 address to the American Physical Society in New York, Vonnegut described his fictional invention of Ice-9 like this:

> I got this lovely idea while I was working as a public-relations man at General Electric. I used to write publicity releases about the research laboratory there, where my brother worked. While there, I heard a story about a visit H. G. Wells had made to the laboratory in the early Thirties.
>
> General Electric was alarmed by the news of his coming. The company told Irving Langmuir, the only Nobel Prize winner in private industry, that he was going to have to entertain Wells. Langmuir didn't want to do it, but he dutifully tried to imagine diversions that would delight Mr. Wells. He made up a science-fiction story he hoped Mr. Wells would want to write. It was about a form of ice that was stable at room temperature. He later died, and so did Langmuir. After Langmuir died, I thought to myself, well, I think maybe I'll write a story.
>
> While I was writing the story about Ice-9, I happened to go to a cocktail party where I was introduced to a crystal-lographer. I told him about this ice which was stable at room temperature. He put his cocktail glass on the mantlepiece. He sat down in an easy chair in the corner. He did not speak to anyone or change expression for half an hour. Then he got up, came back over to the mantlepiece, and picked up his cocktail glass, and he said to me, "Nope." Ice-9 was impossible.

This sounds like Alan, though it could be almost any one of the physicists who were in and out of our house. The following passages from *Cat's Cradle,* though, describe Alan, with an accuracy that's almost spooky, as seen through the eyes of a child:

> "making that cat's cradle was the closest I ever saw my father come to playing what anybody else would call a game. He had no use at all for tricks and games and rules that other people made up. . . .
> "He all of a sudden came out of his study and did something

he'd never done before. He tried to play with me. Not only had he never played with me before; he had hardly ever even spoken to me.

"But he went down on his knees on the carpet next to me, and he showed me his teeth, and he waved that tangle of string in my face. 'See? See? See?' he asked. 'Cat's cradle. See the cat's cradle? See where the pussycat sleeps? Meow. Meow.'

"His pores looked as big as craters on the moon. His ears and nostrils were stuffed with hair. Cigar smoke made him smell like the mouth of Hell. So close up, my father was the ugliest man I had ever seen. . . .

"And then he sang. 'Rockabye catsy, in the tree top'; he sang, 'when the wind blows, the cray-dull will fall. Down will come cray-dull, catsy, and all.'

"I burst into tears. I jumped up and I ran out of the house as fast as I could go."

Like Hoenniker, Alan was so awkward in his attempts to express affection that, for children, his attention bordered on being scary. It was inhuman. When Alan would talk to me, the double-barreled intensity of his gaze, coupled with his curiosity, seemed unnatural. I felt like the subject of an experiment, a fly under a microscope.

The way in which the ocean, in *Cat's Cradle*, crystallizes into "Ice-9", is like the way Alan's polyhedral models imperceptibly and inexorably came to invade our house, until they dominated it. But mostly I remember Alan frowning over his work and knowing that I mustn't interrupt him.

ও

The best side of Alan was when he abandoned his British pretensions in favor of a sly, Yankee wit, a commonsense tone. Alan had always nursed a special fondness for E. B. White's literary style, and as a science writer in his later years Alan perfected a style that, like White's, was urbane and homespun at the same time. But Alan's intellectual style was a virtue for which, in my first seventeen years, I had little use. I longed for a simpler father—someone like Robert Young in *Father Knows Best*—a guy without Alan's slippery irony and without his vanity. I wanted someone corny, tough-talking but loving, proletarian, someone whose face I could read, whose emotions I could understand, someone who liked to watch baseball on TV—who maybe even played in an industrial league. I wanted someone who incarnated so thoroughly and unquestioningly the stereotypical values of American manhood that they'd rub off on me and I'd know, as most of the other boys in the world seemed to, how to act.

I was a scrawny boy, timid and hypersensitive, almost paralyzed with shyness. I could see that somehow, against my will, I had the misfortune to have been born radically different from the other neighborhood kids. They tinkered endlessly with lawnmower engines, building buggies in which to rip around the woods, following the bridle paths. I'd stand sentinel beside two legs in dungarees sticking out from under a car. After an hour or so, I'd quietly slip off, walk home alone and climb the stairs to my room, where I could reread one of Claire Bee's Chip Hilton books or play my 1954 edition of APBA Baseball when Bobby Avila won the American League batting title with a .344 average. If the weather was decent, I might spend another weekend conducting imaginary baseball games alone, hitting my tennis ball into the field. Life in the imagination seemed easier to live alone than with other kids.

Although I didn't know it then, I was much more like Alan than I knew. It was my imagination, not my physical frailty, that made me different from other kids—almost freakishly abnormal. Yet most of the fantasies I cooked up were ones in which I was like Chip Hilton, hypernormal. In my solitary, imaginary baseball league, the better the player, the blander, the more wholesome his name. The two superstars on my team were named Bill Smith and Bob Jones.

৵

If there was any task Alan was unequipped for it was that of showing me or anyone how to be a normal American boy. In order not to feel like a freak, I had to learn boyhood on my own. I studied it. I was a scholar of normality. By the time I entered college, I had come to interpret Alan's inexpressiveness to me as a sign of his infinite forbearance, a sharp sigh of annoyance perpetually withheld, but just barely. His disappointment with me must be so profound it bordered on contempt, contempt for the obvious frivolity of my life—a life devoted exclusively to play, to hitting tennis balls alone into a field and hunting for them, to reading comics.

In 1974, as I was writing my Ph.D. thesis in Boulder, Colorado, my son, Zachary, was born. I had gone ahead, despite Alan's scoffing at the Ph.D., to get one, and when I mentioned to the wife of one of Alan's more celebrated Bell labs colleagues Alan's advice against the doctorate, Lee had cackled with laughter. "Sour grapes!" she declared. Meanwhile, though, I began consciously to put into action my resolution of fifteen years before—to give Zack the kind of attention that Alan had denied me, to give it strategically, with premeditation, like an artist. Or perhaps a better word would be "scientifically"—to give it scientifically.

It seemed that Alan, in his own work habits, had, however inadvertently, taught me something after all. He had shown me by his own example how, if one were truly serious, to undertake a project. It should be planned, like a chemical experiment. One should try to anticipate as many outcomes as possible, even unwanted ones. The Nobel laureate in physics, Richard Feynman, in his book *Surely You're Joking, Mr. Feynman,* in the chapter "Cargo Cult Science," wrote:

> There is *one* feature I notice that is generally missing in cargo cult science. That is the idea that we all hope you have learned studying science in school. . . . It's a kind of scientific integrity, a principle of scientific thought that corresponds to a kind of utter honesty—a kind of leaning over backwards. For example, if you're doing an experiment, you should report everything that you think might make it invalid—not only what you think is right about it: other causes that could possibly explain your results; and things you thought of that you've eliminated by some other experiment, and how they worked—to make sure the other fellow can tell they have been eliminated. . . . The first principle is that you must not fool yourself—and you are the easiest person to fool. So you have to be very careful about that.

Alan's projects had been intellectual, not directly concerned with people. But if one's project were to be a decent parent, mightn't the same kind of forethought be useful? Isn't attention a form of love?

Since birth, I had been imagining fatherhood and construction my own boyhood. Now that I had a son, I found that by putting what I had been studying for so many years into practice, I was able almost wholly to fill the void left by Alan's indifference to me. I found that by being the father that Alan should have been, I could almost magically create, in my own person, the father I had hardly had. I could be father and son at the same time. I could have an ideal father retroactively—a believable fiction—while raising a real son better than myself, a version of myself as I might have been.

I taught Zack to ride a bike exactly as my uncle Jim had taught me, by running alongside the bike and catching it just as it was about to tip over. More tentative, more playful, and far more serious was the ritual of teaching Zack, when he was three, how to throw and to catch a baseball. With a gleam in his eye, he would mimic my theatrical windups, as if he imagined he were scaring me, as if each windup were an omen, a gathering thunderstorm. It wouldn't be lightning that would blow my hand off. It would be something far more terrible— his fastball—a thing of limitless potential. Before my eyes, I watched Zack discover, understand, then practice the advantages of imagination:

Catch with My Son

It's evening
out on the slovenly lawn
as he tries to connect us
with a straight line.
But the loose thing
has no sense of direction.
It gets snarled in the grass.
I hold it up again
in the soft remnants of sun
for him to see
and pull it taut,
take aim, hint

what I could do with it.
Draw a bead on the walnut tree.
Blow his head off cleanly.
I wind up again
slowly
like stroking a knife
on a whetstone, *silk*
silk, till the edge
of the edge is out of sight
and the skin on the thumb
drawn against it
shudders. I wind up
again, then roll
it to him.
He balances it
like a spear
between us carefully
aligning the air.
He's laughing.
A line sings
through my head. A line
goes through my hand.
Giggling,
he winds up again
but does not throw.
The line will go anywhere
he wants, this
is better than throwing.

In my experience, intellectual superiority, for all its glamor, is hardly ever nice. In his essay "Technically Sweet," based on a remark by Oppenheimer that the solution to the manufacture of the atomic bomb was "Technically Sweet," the poet Reg Saner expressed poignantly, in both personal and universal terms, the moral dilemma of intellectuality:

> If on this serene afternoon I ask myself about inner distances and outer ones, their causes—like answers that open on questions—keep disappearing into each other. Oppie's wounds

and ambitions. Hitler's childhood. The admirable, astonishing persistence of Madame Curie. Allure of the technically sweet. The ruinous pleasures of ego. Indeed, doesn't my own egotism, like all long-range weaponry, depend on the illusion of distance?

Not long ago, I had dinner with a group of physicists in Los Alamos. Suddenly I was surrounded by all the shoptalk I had grown up with. My hosts were scoffing bitterly at the supercollider project in Texas. Nothing but a great boondoggle, they said grimly, knowingly; though they were sure that the physicist in charge would eventually get the Nobel.

I listened attentively, thinking "sour grapes," thinking how many times I'd listened to this same conversation as a child, and to similar discussions in my own field of endeavor, about the MacArthur Fellowship, the Pulitzer Prize. And I wondered for the nth time at the deadly, addictive charm of intellectuality, at the vanity that goes with it—at Alan's unlimited vanity, and my own.

Peyton Place

In the fall of 1958, as my brother and I were beginning our senior year in high school, our Westminster Youth Fellowship, under the guidance of Reverend Knierman, began a debate that would eventually occupy the entire school year. The issue seemed urgent: "how far the girl should let the boy go." The benchmarks for "distance" were the words "necking" and "petting." A book called *The Facts of Life and Love for Teenagers* published by the YMCA in 1956 had coined these innovative-sounding terms, and illustrated them by means of little parables. Quite a few of them used driving as a metaphor for sex. Here is a typical passage from chapter 12, "That Question of Petting":

> John and Mary went out for a date in John's car. John began to drive very fast. Mary began to feel breathless and scared. She said to John, "I think we're going too far too fast." So John stopped pushing on the accelerator, and they were able to slow up in time to avoid an accident. How relieved they were to arrive home safely.

Or, as Jimmy Connon, one of the neighborhood kids I played with, solemnly reported his mother had said to him: It was dangerous to touch a girl's breasts because they could go crazy, "They can go out of control, like cars."

As the debate toiled on in our fellowship group, there emerged various distinctions. "Light necking" could lead to "moderate necking," which could, in turn, lead to "heavy necking." There was "light petting," "moderate petting," and

From the *Laurel Review,* forthcoming.

"heavy petting." There was petting "above the waist" and pet-ting "below the waist." The issue of petting sparked the most debate, because it had so many categories. As our debate contin-ued into the spring, it grew so technical it sounded legalistic— "moderate to heavy necking without French kissing"; "light to moderate petting above the waist"—or like a weather report: "moderate to heavy winds off Montauk Point." Led painstak-ingly ahead by Reverend Knierman, we finally agreed that it was wrong to "go all the way" before marriage, but that "heavy petting below the waist" was probably okay "if the girl really loved the boy."

Our real sex education, however, came not from church but from the novel *Peyton Place*, by Grace Metalious. Published in 1956, the same year as Allen Ginsberg's scandalous poem *Howl*, the jacket claimed that this was a book that "lifts the lid off a small New England town." I know it's hard to believe from our superior, "liberated" vantage point of the 1990s, but *Peyton Place* created a sensation. Its descriptions of sexual acts between ordinary people were, for those repressed times, much franker than what people were used to. The descrip-tions were written in a tone that I would characterize as "ear-nest dirtiness" or, perhaps, "lustful sanctimony." Both the book's prurience and its ugly style are foreshadowed in its very opening sentences:

> Indian summer is like a woman. Ripe, hotly passionate, but fickle, she comes and goes as she pleases so that one is never sure whether she will come at all, nor for how long she will stay. In northern New England, Indian summer puts up a scarlet-tipped hand to hold winter back for a little while. She brings with her the time of the last warm spell, an uncharted season which lives until Winter moves in with its backbone of ice and accoutrements of leafless trees and hard frozen ground.

These sentences, with their corny personifications and their pretentious diction ("accoutrements" indeed!) are like the writings of a bright high-school senior trying to impress and perhaps even shock some Victorian schoolmarm. In the black-and-white photo on the back of the jacket, Metalious— "this Pandora in blue jeans"—is seated before her Royal

Standard, brooding. She is wearing a plaid wool hunting jacket. Her face is heavy, homely, rather sad—the face of a wallflower.

By 1959, my brother and I had practically memorized all "the good parts" in *Peyton Place*. We had turned to them so many times that we could find them by rotating the book ninety degrees from reading position. The compressed page-ends of our paperbacks looked like a club sandwich. They were laminated—layers of white and tan. The tan layers were the good parts. We referred to them by page number. We knew the page numbers by heart. There was page 124—Betty Anderson and Rodney Harrington in the car:

> ''Come on, Betty," whispered Rodney. "Come on."
>
> "No," she said petulantly. "I won't. I'm mad at you."
>
> "Aw, come on, Betty. Don't be like that. Kiss me."
>
> "No," said Betty, tossing her head. "Go get skinny Allison MacKenzie to kiss you. She's the one you brought to the dance." . . .
>
> "Aw, come on, Betty. Don't be like that. Kiss me a little."
>
> Betty lifted her head and Rodney quickly covered her mouth with his. She could kiss, thought Rodney, like no one else in the world. She didn't kiss with just her lips, but with her teeth and her tongue, and all the while she made noises deep in her throat, and her fingernails dug into his shoulders.
>
> "Oh, honey, honey," whispered Rodney, and that was all he could say before Betty's tongue went between his teeth again.
>
> Her whole body twisted and moved when he kissed her, and when his hands found their way to her breasts, she moaned as if she were hurt. She writhed on the seat until she was lying down, with only her legs and feet not touching him, and Rodney fitted his body to her without taking his mouth from hers.
>
> "Is it up, Rod?" she panted, undulating her body under his. "Is it up good and hard?"
>
> "Oh, yes," he whispered, almost unable to speak. "Oh, yes."
>
> Without another word, Betty jacknifed her knees, pushed Rodney away from her, clicked the lock on the door and was outside the car.
>
> "Now go shove it into Allison MacKenzie," she screamed at him. "Go get the girl you brought to the dance and get rid of it with her!"

You would think it would be impossible to be *both* naive and dirty at the same time. *Dirtiness* implies some kind of sly knowingness, a snicker. But the passage above is naive. *And* it is dirty.

The best-known "good part" is probably on page 203, the "hurry, hurry, hurry" scene with Betty and Rodney at the beach.

> For only a moment, Rodney was panicky, and after that he did not care, not even when she had to help him. For less than a moment he wondered if all the stories he had read and heard about virgins could be wrong. Betty did not scream in pain or beg him to stop hurting her. She led him without a fumble, and her hips moved quickly, expertly. She did not cry out at all. She moaned deep in her throat the way she did when he kissed her, and the only word she uttered was, "Hurry. Hurry. Hurry."
>
> After that, Rodney did not notice what she did and said. He was lost in her, drowning in her, and he did not think at all. In a very few minutes he lay shivering on the blanket next to her, and her voice seemed to be coming from very far away.
>
> "Smart guy," she was hissing at him. "Smart guy who knew all about it. So smart he doesn't even know enough to wear a safe. Get me home, you dumb jackass. Quick!"

A more significant scene in the book takes place between Allison MacKenzie's mother, Constance, and her husband, Tom, on page 278.

> "Do it to me then."
>
> He raised his head and smiled down into her face. "Do what?" he teased. "Tell me."
>
> "You know."
>
> "No, tell me. What do you want me to do to you?" She looked up at him appealingly.
>
> "Say it," he said. "Say it." She whispered the words in his ear and his fingers dug into her shoulders.
>
> "Like this?"
>
> "Please," she said. "Please." And then, "Yes! Yes, yes, yes."
>
> Later she lay with her head on his shoulder and one hand flat against his chest.
>
> "For the first time in my life I'm not ashamed afterward," she said.

But what exactly did Constance say? My guess is that it was in the imperative and consisted of two words—a verb that begins with the letter *F,* followed by the direct object, "me." Of course, this is only a conjecture; but from the vantage point of today the absence of the "F-word" in this scene is of historical interest. The book's setting, the 1950s, is legendary for its political and sexual repression. It was a time when many more adult, white, middle-class women than now had been taught to be ashamed of sexual intercourse, a time so prissy that it was actually illegal to publish the word *fuck* in a book. The scene with Constance and Tom dramatizes neatly but inadvertently how censorship in the public domain was reflected in people's private lives. Is Constance reluctant to say "fuck" because the book is not allowed to print the word? Or is that putting the cart before the horse? Does public censorship spring from individual repression and reflect *that?* The former, I think. Even in the private domain, the roots of censorship are political.

ɝ

In the 1950s, before the bombshell of *Peyton Place,* my expectations about sex were formed from movies and television. In those days, experiments with what we thought was sex were conducted in the dark, usually at the movies. My first kiss was with a girl named Sally. I was thirteen. According to junior-high-school protocol in 1954, if a girl didn't kiss you by your third date, she probably never would. My mother had dropped Sally and me off at the Community Theatre, in Morristown, New Jersey, to watch the movie *Battle Cry,* starring Aldo Ray. By the time the main feature began, Sally and I had progressed through various stages of holding hands—first her left hand in my right, then my left hand on top of her left hand on top of my right, then her right hand coming around on top of my left hand, on top of her left hand on top of my right. We were beyond the "hands" stage. My right arm was around her, and her head was on my right shoulder. Silhouetted directly in front of us a couple was necking vigorously, the boy's head like a vampire's lolling over her head, feeding so sloppily that the very thought of so much saliva gave me pause. But there remained the problem of how to cross the gap between my face and Sally's. Very tentatively, by mutual consent, we negotiated the distance. Her lips were dry, slightly crusted, "scarred battle-grounds," as I described them later to my brother. In the distance, from the movie sound track, I could hear artillery firing. I felt some regret that I was missing it; but my present business was more important—a *real* adventure—and as her eyelashes grazed my cheek, I was astonished. This was like landing on the moon. The strangeness, the otherness of the landscape of a girl's face was a terrain so unstable that it might not support a person's weight. The territory was utterly alien, new. Sally's kiss wasn't sexy. But sex wasn't the point. Kissing girls was a boy-hood adventure. Sally Adams, Harriet Russell, Katherine Simko. Just as I kept a list of all the different types of military jets I had actually seen, I began to keep a list of the girls I had actually kissed.

The summer I was fifteen, Mrs. Wood, Alan's colleague in the Bell labs, had a niece, Lois Reager, visit her from California. Mrs. Wood had no children. To keep her niece entertained, she introduced Lois to me, and I took her on the Erie-Lackawanna railroad to New York City for a tour of the UN building and, later, the Circle Tour by boat around Manhattan Island. Lois was going to be in New Jersey for three weeks. It was a lot of time to kill. One afternoon, I had Lois over to watch TV in the "playroom." My parents discreetly closed the doors to the play-room, and Lois and I practiced necking, a kind of tender nuzzling—closed-mouthed kissing during which we angled our heads as we had seen people do in movies and on TV. It was like nuzzling a dog's tiny, cool nose. It wasn't turgid, but it wasn't unpleasant, either. It was sort of interesting. The most satisfying moments were the glimpses I caught (when I opened my eyes) of Lois's face, its expression of conventional abandon. Everything was by the book: head back, eyes closed. We were acting. It was like being in a scene in the movies, and I found this very reassuring. I knew what we looked like *right now,* and our posture was correct—the official posture. Her sigh—certifiably conventional—was icing on the cake.

One of my favorite TV shows that summer was called *The Bob Cummings Show.* Bob Cummings played an oily, handsome, young fashion photographer juggling a collection of beautiful models. In each episode, one of the models would begin to feel slighted by Bob, jealous of one of the other models. Bob's task was, while carrying on a serious flirtation with whichever model he'd picked out, to make sure that all the rest of his girls felt equally special. He managed this by flashing his smile, by tossing off a few vague promises, and by dispensing little favors of fussy physical attention as to a studio of poodles. He measured out strategic doses of flattery. The trick was to keep as many beautiful girls as possible on the hook at once, a kind of fraternity sport.

The most interesting character on the show was Bob's secretary, "Shultzie." Shultzie was a foil for the models. Bob's girls were in their twenties, Shultzie was maybe forty-five. The girls' faces were pinups, clichés of beauty. Shultzie was homely. She wore a mousy suit. Her graying hair was pinned up in a bun. Shultzie had a permanent crush on Bob, and Bob's task was to resist her advances without hurting her feelings, to keep her on the string, even though he'd never touch her with a ten-foot pole.

As the girls cooed and murmured around Bob like beauty queens, Shultzie would roll her eyes, raise her eyebrows, and grin sardonically. Her art was irony. She accepted the fact that she was, by definition—her age and appearance—the butt of an unspoken joke. All her ironic cues made it clear that she would gladly accept that role, so long as she could remain in the vicinity of Bob.

At the end of each show, when the misunderstanding between the two rivals for Bob's attention had been cleared up, Bob would draw the girl he'd been angling for all along into his arms, and they would earnestly, mechanically, with their mouths closed, fasten their lips together and freeze in that posture for a few seconds. If this was "sex," it was completely sanitized—sex without saliva. It was no less difficult to imagine Vice President Richard Nixon abandoning himself with a woman, "lost in her, drowning in her," than to imagine Harriet Nelson (the wife of Ozzie), moaning "deep in her throat. . . 'Hurry. Hurry. Hurry.'"

By the time I was a senior in high school, I had been trained by movies and TV to believe that the ideal way to treat girls was the way Bob Cummings did, by means of breezy, patronizing, manipulation—that charm was just technique, a collection of "moves" or "lines." I believed that one could and should live one's life without emotion. That's what adulthood *was*. To be a man and a grown-up, all you had to do was what my father had done: become very good at something. I could be like my orthodontist, Dr. Swain, with his navy crew cut: brisk, cheery, a technician—utterly efficient, utterly competent, without emotion. Emotion was childish. Emotion was clearly an inconvenience.

Occasionally, though, a bit of reality, like a piece of soot in the eye, would blow in and irritate the suburban perfection. One such intrusion was Marcella Grillo. Marcella was from Brazil and a friend of a girl, Aimee Meier, in my class at Far Brook School. Full-lipped and dark-haired, Marcella was twenty years old and living in Washington, D.C., where her parents were with the diplomatic corps. Because the Meiers lived in Chatham, ten miles away, Stephen and I had to endure the humiliation of asking my parents to drive us to pick Aimee and Marcella up, bring them home, and later drive them back. Our "date" with them would be to sit and talk in the playroom, then perhaps to play some 45 rpm records and dance. Dancing would be a legitimate excuse for physical contact.

The evening was stilted. Only Marcella, who was a poised, cosmopolitan woman among children, had anything to say. With her heavy lips and swarming, pitch-black hair, she seemed exotic. At length, we decided to go outside for a walk. The night was tropical. Scent of honeysuckle, wisteria. It was the kind of night that, for my entire adolescence, seemed to demand some kind of sexual completion. Wasn't that what such nights were *for*?

As we walked, Stephen and Marcella lagged farther and farther behind. I walked very slowly, simply to kill time. There was nothing to say. I took about forty-five minutes, dawdling on Pleasantville Road. When Aimee and I finally returned to the house, Stephen and Marcella hadn't arrived, so we sat forlornly until, perhaps half an hour later, they strolled in. We all agreed that it was time to take Aimee and Marcella back to the Meiers'.

Alone upstairs, Stephen and I compared notes about the evening. As he described to me her incredible, endless French-kissing, I was racked with jealousy; but I was also annoyed. What right did Stephen have, who had played mainly with girls in grade school as if he were one of them, to poach on my territory, to hog something that he didn't care that much about, something that may even have mildly disgusted him? Even more dismaying, he told me that Marcella had felt sorry for him, how she had, in a sorrowful maternal tone, whispered over and over, "You poor boy." It seemed such a waste. Why was it so much easier for Stephen to attract girls than it was for me, who *really* wanted them? In retrospect, the answer is obvious. He had, from his eccentricity—his effeminacy—acquired the habit of emotional honesty. He didn't have a "line." He was the opposite of Bob Cummings. He had a soul that he was willing to share.

I had a soul too, of course. But being a careful conformist, I prided myself on being as inauthentic as possible, on behavior that would entail the least risk, the lowest emotional cost. I would park with my date, we'd make some small talk, and then we'd fall silent. After awhile, in a puzzled, serious voice, I'd ask, "Have you ever experienced real ecstasy?"

The girl, immediately interested in the subject, would stop and think and then begin to unveil secret experiences ("I've never told anybody this"). The talk would continue, very serious and halting, and, invariably, the girl would say something like, "I *like* talking with you. Most guys don't like to talk. They're only after one thing." I knew what she meant. Wasn't this burst of intimacy the preface to her putting her head on my shoulder?

No, she'd rather talk. I couldn't blame her. I was so skinny I hardly had a shoulder. I was like Shultzie, an outsider. I was a complete wimp. I waxed my crew cut religiously, and when, in *Picnic*, the desperately horny high-school teacher played by Rosalind Russell, pawing compulsively at William Holden, ripped his shirt off, my reaction was orthodox: shock.

Throughout most of the 1950s, I had worn braces on my teeth—the ultimate suburban badge of identification. The regimen of braces had seemed endless, but I believed my mother when she assured me that nice straight teeth would make me popular with girls. Looking back on the 1950s, it seems as if I spent the entire decade in a dentist's chair being "straightened."

ે●

In retrospect, the coincidence of sexual repression and political repression such as McCarthyism seems inevitable. Both forms of repression involve devaluation and discrediting the inner life of the individual. In the mid-1950s, the inner life was treated as a civil threat. Flickering throughout books of imaginative literature set in the 1950s there is the motif of electroshock therapy. It's prominent in Kesey's *One Flew Over the Cuckoo's Nest*, in Sylvia Plath's *The Bell Jar*, and in Ginsberg's *Howl*, a poem that, in its historical context, is preeminently a dramatization of the inner life of the individual finally breaking out heroically against official permission, in the full knowledge that those who dare to display their suppressed inner lives in the open may be branded insane and consigned to "the concrete void of insulin metrasol electricity hydrotherapy psychotherapy occupational therapy pingpong & amnesia" while, as Sylvia Plath grimly put it in "Lady Lazarus" about her suicide attempts, "The peanut-crunching crowd /Shoves in to see." Under such political conditions, the devalued "inner life" is like a sideshow, and those who pause to behold it in a public arena, whether they like it or not, find themselves in the position of being voyeuristic spectators.

In *Howl*, what Ginsberg called "the best minds of my generation" were those

who balled in the morning in the evenings in rosegardens and the grass of public parks and cemeteries scattering their semen freely to whomever come who may,
. . . .
Who copulated ecstatic and insatiate with a bottle of beer a sweetheart a package of cigarettes a candle and fell off the bed, and continued along the floor and down the hall and ended fainting on the wall with a vision of ultimate cunt and come eluding the last gyzym of consciousness.

In what sense were they "the best?" They were "the best minds," because, despite all the civic propaganda about the dangers of "going too far too fast," they recognized the value of the inner life. They insisted on expressing it even though to do so was against the rules.

In 1959, the year I discovered the good parts of *Peyton Place* and read Ginsberg's *Howl* with a suburban shudder of revulsion, I finally, with the maternal encouragement of a high-school friend, screwed up the courage to slip my hand under her blouse and cup like a trophy one of her whalelike breasts—to try for a curious minute or so "light petting above the waist."

A War Baby Looks Back

In the tender years of Eisenhower's first
term, I started mine
in Dr. Swain's office, my jaws pried wide,
my gums stuffed with cotton cigarettes,
staring sadly up into a soft, fluorescent
light while Dr. Swain peered down in
and frowned. I had to wear elastic bands
that caught in my mouth on steel hooks;
to wash my abhorrent, plastic bite-plate
off each night until my teeth were
straight. It was all worth it.
Thanks to Dr. Swain, one spring evening
toward the end of Eisenhower's second
term, on the cold leather of my parents'
car, a girl named Tina
let me feel her up.

But for years afterward, "sex," like the word itself, remained for me a pleasure associated both with feelings of furtiveness and defiance. "Sex," in that lubricious, slightly embarrassed sense of the word, may be one of the idiosyncracies of my generation. When, a freshman in college, I lost my virginity, it was not a joyous experience. There was soot in it, a mark that most everybody I know who came of age sexually in the

1950s seems still to bear from the attempts of American government—of both church and state—to police American middle-class sexual behavior, a mark connected ultimately with McCarthyism. For those of us who believed our government's sexual propaganda and internalized it, it was, I can see now, the equivalent of taking the Fifth Amendment. Even now, many of us, like Metalious's Constance MacKenzie, occasionally marvel to ourselves, "I'm not ashamed."

American Anaesthetics

Ever since my graduation from Morristown High School, I've tried to live as though those three years, like a term in the state pen, never happened. But when you're raising kids, you discover, sooner or later, that this kind of denial is impossible. Our kids make us relive all the phases of our lives when we were their age. To make sure that we do this: it's one of their jobs.

If we're lucky, most of these relivings are joyous. I remember teaching my daughter, Alanna, how to tie her shoe, how to stay up on a two-wheel bike, how to drive a car—each time reliving with an intensely pleasing sense of recognition and completion the experience of learning those things myself. I could reexperience vicariously the profound aesthetic satisfaction of "catching on" how to do it, of "getting it." And when as a high-school sophomore Alanna was a state champion swimmer in breaststroke, I was awed at her physical strength, exultant at her victories—more exultant even than she was.

But not all relivings are like that. The reliving of childhood is apt to be joyous, but not the reliving of adolescence. Two years later, Alanna started smoking cigarettes and hanging out with a seedier crowd. I watched her begin to copy her new girlfriends. I didn't like them. With their phony, goodie-good politeness to grown ups—a parody of politeness, really—and their mirthless, calculated giggles and their layers of makeup, there was something helpless, exploitable about them. They resembled a bunch of silly starlets in blonde wigs on some TV quiz show. They had no taste in boyfriends, in cars, or in

From *Many Mountains Moving,* inaugural issue (December 1994).

clothes. Without knowing it, they were ludicrous. And suddenly all the pathetic lengths to which I'd gone in high school to be attractive to girls returned to me, as raw, as bitterly embarrassing as if I'd graduated yesterday instead of thirty years ago. The memories made me angry, because they made me ashamed—not of Alanna and her friends, who didn't know any better—but of myself and of the culture in which we are raised. It's there on television: soap opera for the girls, football for the boys. It's high school all over again. To understand America, one need only remember high school.

Even when Alanna was a star athlete, before she decided to try to be like everybody else, she was watching soap operas. I watched her watch them. She watched them studiously, as if preparing herself for something. Every afternoon, as if to attend her favorite class, she'd show up on time to study *The Young and the Restless*. All summer. Of course, it was also summer on the screen. But the grown-ups on the screen never went outdoors. There were more important things to do. They would talk about these things, talk and talk in low, confidential voices about each other.

Somebody was getting a divorce. Some young punk was threatening his bride. There was a beautiful young woman sobbing. The scene changed to another beautiful young couple. They were face to face. They looked enrapt. "I love you," the blonde whispered. "I love you," said the man, quietly. "I love you," the blonde whispered. They sounded like people at a funeral.

But with a rapt solemnity Alanna was studying them. She was taking mental notes. She was memorizing them. The class was *How to Be a Woman*. The scene was fading, and the theme song—*Doom* / doom! ... *Doom* / doom!—had already returned, like an inexorable heartbeat, a kind of hymn confirming the universality of sorrow. And now the violins came in. They swelled. *You're not a- /lone!* We were being encouraged to let our hair down and wail.

No sooner had the violins faded into the lunch-hour commercial than Alanna would be on the phone with her friends. It was her homework. She was practicing her giggle. She was practicing how not to sound too smart or too critical of anything, how to be like everybody else. She was practicing for the real world, the world in all its sorrows which on TV, even to me, looked almost thrilling.

But the sorrows of the real world are all too easy.

ॐ

At exactly the same age as my daughter, I too had begun my self-guided course in how to smoke a cigarette. I took up smoking because I thought it would make me look glamorous. I remember watching—even studying—the way Lawrence Harvey and Simone Signoret smoked in the movie *Room at the Top*. When Harvey placed two cigarettes in his mouth, lit both, then handed one of them to her (slightly moistened), it seemed to me to be a grandly sophisticated, Old World gesture, a gesture I immediately began to practice with my girlfriend, Georgia.

Huddled together, lost in a small college in the seedy wilds of Ohio, we practiced the "French inhale," and felt immeasurably world-weary, invested with a faded, slightly jaded glamor. Camus and French existentialism were, at the time, all the vogue. In every single photograph, Camus, with his haunted Humphrey Bogart countenance, had a cigarette in his mouth. It was a fixture; it was Camus's signature. With the help of a cigarette, the Popcorn Bowl in Oberlin, Ohio, could be like a stage set, some dim café on the Left Bank or in Morocco. In a secondhand store I bought a tattered army surplus jacket. It was way too big for me. It draped limply from my skinny frame like a piece of human clothing on an insect. I didn't care. The insect had returned home after fighting, in its imagination, against the Fascists in the Spanish Civil War. With a pack of Camels, Georgia and I could pretend that we had lived through all the scenes we'd witnessed in the movies. We'd been through the Occupation, through World War II.

To pretend to be Humphrey Bogart in *Casablanca* is harmless enough, I guess. It's an attempt to import into a bland suburban life a little seasoning, a little style. But what is style *for?* Style doesn't exist only for itself. Style is a language. The practice of style—a public gesture—is fundamentally a method of counteracting the threat of loneliness and of isolation. Like language, style is how an individual expresses his or her sense of place in a community. Whether you're an adult driving a Corvette, an adolescent lighting a Camel cigarette, or a little boy wearing a Batman costume on Halloween, you're using style deliberately to make a statement. The costume, the mask may vary; but the statement is always the same: *I am not being left out.*

By the time you're a junior or senior in high school, the terror of being left out can be almost pathological. As I witnessed my daughter almost beside herself with excitement on a Friday or Saturday night before a party, I cringed inside, remembering things I would just as soon forget. In high school, Saturday night was like an approaching final exam. The exam wasn't in Algebra. Its subject matter was more basic. The test question: *Are you being left out? Is there some big party to which everybody else has been invited except you?* It is a question many people never get over.

I haven't. I still sometimes on Saturday night catch myself wondering a little worriedly if I shouldn't be out somewhere, doing something. I have friends who, when they feel this way, drive to the nearest mall to go "shopping." They're not looking for any item in particular. They're going to hang out. They feel better simply to be in the presence of merchandise, aisles and aisles of it, a wilderness of gaily colored trinkets—as if the merchandise itself were crowds of people. It's a kind of party. Shopping is a party for the lonely.

In high school, the test of whether you're being left out or not is sexual. Being desired like a piece of merchandise is a test of your market value in the world. The "store" in which products are publicly evaluated is the high-school football stadium. When poor little Billy Connolly, a fearless 125-pound urchin who was a first-string linebacker for Morristown High, could be found like a terrier at the bottom of almost every pileup hanging on to some giant running-back's shoe, when he would several times a game be helped limping off the field and five minutes later, taped up, race back out for some more punishment, he was trying blindly, in the only way he knew, to be desired. Not just by girls. He was trying to be desired by the world.

James Wright's little poem, "Autumn Begins in Martins Ferry, Ohio," a poem organized like a syllogism, is all about this, but it goes further. It presents high-school football as a ritual reflecting not only the exploitation of boys by football, but the exploitation of women by men, the exploitation of men by industry, the exploitation of blacks by whites—the exploitation and eventual ruin of nature itself by organized commercial power, leaving human refuse in its wake in bars, gray-faced, "ruptured," "ashamed."

> In the Shreve high football stadium,
> I think of Polacks nursing long beers in Tiltonville,
> And gray faces of Negroes in the blast furnace at
>   Benwood,
> And the ruptured nightwatchman of Wheeling Steel,
> Dreaming of heroes.
>
> All the proud fathers are ashamed to go home.
> Their women cluck like starved pullets,
> Dying for love.
>
> Therefore,
> Their sons grow suicidally beautiful
> At the beginning of October,
> And gallop terribly against each other's bodies.

As Wright's poem accurately shows, this exploitation begins in high school. It is in high school in America where, in their instinctive drive to be desired by the world, people "grow suicidally beautiful."

Are you desirable? Does the world desire you? Same question. In America, Saturday night is when this crude question gets inevitable. Anything to stem the anxiety that you might somehow be missing out. *What* you might be missing out on is never clear. Adolescent and adult loneliness is only part sexual ache. It's deeper. It's archetypal—a need to be where the action is. I think that it is to be with the species—a member of the human species.

ஐ

In suburban New Jersey at night the lights from the New York metropolitan area, like the light from a distant midway, or perhaps a war, make a low blaze along the skyline. It's as if a great party is in session somewhere just over the horizon, and in 1959 this party was being conducted by the passionate voice of Alan Freed on WINS radio, dedicating songs—*From Jeanine and Paula at Mel's Candystore to Dickie and Bobbie and all the guys at Tony's Diner on Amsterdam and 106th St. Elvis Presley and, "Love me, Tender"!*

"Tony's Diner." I cursed my luck to have been born with a stupid name like *Jonathan,* and with thin lips, frizzy "dishwater blond" hair (as a girl named Lois called it) instead of with a name like *Tony* and with heavy, sensual lips and thick, black, Latin hair that could be greased in a "ducktail" like Elvis's. How did you join the party?

In my senior year in high school I found the crowd that I'd been seeking: a kid from Blair Academy, named Reynolds Dodd; a kid from Bayley-Ellard (the local Catholic parochial high school), named Richie Bertleson; and a kid from Chatham High, named Danny Koeck. Unlike the careful, competitive kids in my advanced college-prep classes at Morristown, these guys were interested in nothing except girls, cars, and booze. Dodd had his own car, a Bonneville. He did most of the driving. Sometimes my brother came with us. Sometimes we were joined by Crick Hatch. Crick had flunked out of Deerfield Academy. He had black locks and a face like the Hollywood star Robert Wagner. It was the most beautiful face any of us had ever seen, and whenever Crick was with us, we attracted attention. It was as if we were driving a brand-new white Corvette or a Thunderbird. We felt glamorous. But it wasn't our car. And it wasn't our looks. It was Crick. His presence put us in Hollywood.

On Saturday nights, we drove. There was no self-contained block to cruise as in the movie *American Graffiti.* There was nothing but the waste of northern New Jersey, a concrete tundra of highways going over or past residential areas, warehouses, factories, airports, business districts, railroads, roadhouses lit up like Christmas trees, semitrailers lit up like Christmas trees, bridges lit up like Christmas trees, Christmas at midsummer in all directions, a bewilderment of moving lights, diesel fumes, concrete dividers.

We drove. And we drove. And drove. And we drove, it was as if by simply covering distance you could accomplish something. In a sense, we did. We were using up time. Although we had no destination, we were consuming distance. We were shoppers, consumers. Many older people, I've noticed, eat out of boredom. They eat in order to fill time. It gives them a vague feeling of accomplishment. There's something terribly American about this—to consume food you don't need or especially want simply in order to have something to do.

At seventeen, we were too itchy to sit still and eat. We consumed something else. We consumed the commodity of distance: which is rate multiplied by time. Which is pure emptiness. So long as we were moving, we could be a part of it, pure products of America going crazy, anonymous. We could be what we had always wanted to be—*like anybody.*

I'd zip the seal off a pack of Camels, tear back a square opening to reveal them like a nest of cartridges, and whack it against my other hand to force one or two up, slide one out, open my Zippo with a flick of the wrist, with a snick of the thumb get flame, and then—the best part—a flourish, flicking the Zippo shut: *snap.* I'd practiced these moves in the mirror like a U.S. marshall practicing his draw, until I was certain I looked like a veteran. I had my part down pat. To inhale and exhale smoke and stare out the windshield, empty, appraising, at the night. To be simply another guy, something as abstract as an army private, a unit.

Saturday nights were improvisational. We'd start off driving somewhere—maybe to Chatham to pick up Koeck, or past some girl's house, then we'd have to invent another destination. Usually it was the state line. In New York State, you could buy booze at the age of eighteen. We'd drive the ugly thirty miles to Staten Island, across the Goethals Bridge and hit the first package store we saw, popping the cans as we peeled out of the parking lot, drinking as hard as we could.

If Dodd's parents weren't home, we'd go there and play tribal games like "Thumper." One night a friend of Koeck's, a pudgy greaser named Jimmy Delasandro, came with us. Back at Dodd's we all chipped in to bet Jimmy that he couldn't drink a quart of port in three minutes. Bertleson and Dodd gravely ushered Jimmy outside. The rest of us waited in the kitchen. In a few minutes, they all trooped back in. Jimmy had won his bet—small change, really, less than five dollars. After about ten minutes, Jimmy began to get animated, flushed. He broke into a sweat. Suddenly he was dizzy, and Koeck and Dodd, like two concerned nurses, helped him outside and released him. He became a pig foundering on all fours on the lawn. Liquid seemed to spout from every one of his bodily orifices at once. He struggled somehow to a lawnchair and passed out. Dodd tucked a blanket around him

From his friends at Blair, Dodd had heard about a strip-joint called the Heat Wave in the Village. We took the Holland Tunnel. The Heat Wave was below street level. It was loud and dim with smoke. A leering middle-aged man in a tuxedo introduced the "girls." I ordered a sloe gin fizz. The "girls" were hardened, embittered looking. They were maybe the age of my mother, maybe even a little older. Their necks had creases. Their breasts were veined. Their tits were menacing. They were like cobras without fangs, cobras with false teeth. They'd select a customer, pull his head between their breasts and whip their breasts side to side around his ears.

I was careful to sit far enough back from the stage area that I would not be touched, but Crick, with his perfect black locks and his long-lashed eyes, took a front-row seat. When the cobra-lady had worked her way to him, she grinned at him—a serpent's grin. Her lips were thin, it was more a grimace than a grin.

"What abut you, Sonny?"

Crick leered up at her. "I'm afraid."

The club erupted with laughter. Then she gave it to him. And I knew that Crick was probably the coolest guy I'd ever met.

Those Saturday nights cruising New Jersey, sometimes, if we happened to pass a young couple walking hand in hand, we'd thrust our collective puss out the window and yell, "Go ahead, *fuck* her! *I* did!" Then Dodd peeled out, and we'd all whoop and congratulate each other. Whenever I'm searching to understand what could be going through the minds of high-school boys, what I remind myself is this: As we shouted

"Go ahead, fuck her, I did," *I was positive it was the coolest thing I had ever done.*

Sometimes, on a two-lane highway, Dodd would speed up to ninety miles an hour and, if there were an oncoming car, he'd deliberately swerve at it, cut back into the right lane at the last split second. I should have been terrified, but I felt nothing. It wouldn't be cool.

One night we were returning from a New York sortie. It was well after 3 A.M. Dodd, the driver as usual, was uncommonly silent. Everybody in the car was drunk, nodding off, except for me in the front and my brother in the back. Dodd was perspiring as he squinted forward with a sullen, maniacal concentration. Trees were flashing on either side of us, almost swiping the windows. We were in Jockey Hollow National Monument, on a one-lane black top. Dodd started accelerating: eighty, ninety, a flat one hundred miles an hour. I heard a cry from behind me, like the scream of a puppy. My brother, my identical twin brother, Stephen, was curled on the floor, sobbing with terror.

"Shut up!" I snarled down at him. Stephen had the reputation of being a sissy. I would *not* be compromised by it.

That was the absolute low point in my determination *not to be left out*—unforgivable. It was the full measure of what I didn't know. The organic numbness of adolescence is the numbness of a lynch-mob. You don't know anything. You don't feel anything. You don't fear anything. You've been anaesthetized. But it was who we were then.

૨**ઢ**

Most middle-class Americans never entirely leave their adolescence. Why? It may be because, in America, we can economically afford it. Adolescence is a luxury. And it's good for business. Business not only supports adolescence. Business fosters it. To a significant extent, business lives off it. American television, with its diet of anaesthetics—soap operas and quiz shows on weekdays for the girls, football and basketball on weekends for the boys—is our own adolescence recycled and sold back to us, an eternal present tense of consuming everything in sight and heaving the remains out the car window and leaving it for junk. Our own adolescence has been so shrewdly and deliberately marketed on such a stupendous scale that it is our national ideology. Since the end of World War II, America had come to resemble one great, crass, hard-drinking, pill-popping, football-crazy public high school, cars peeling out of the parking lot, cheerleaders flouncing and shouting, selling us national spirit, while the somber coaches (in the Pentagon), recruiting for the coming season, roll artillery up Main Street every Fourth of July.

The anaesthetic inner landscape of America permeates so thoroughly the outer that we are no longer conscious of it: we take it for granted. The two landscapes are intimately related: the places where people go for fast, illicit, one-way, disposable pleasures are always junked. The following poem recalls a beach on Lake Erie where as college students we used to go to have "beach parties." The poem is set in 1962. Lake Erie has since been cleaned up, but thirty years ago, it was so polluted by industrial waste that it had been pronounced "dead."

Junk

Dim, heavy Ginny, whose wet mouth
which smelled like a washcloth
I joked about next morning
driving south as if
I were leaving this behind—
these words are more
to remind *me* than you:
that dusk when I drove us
to Lake Erie *did* happen.
Those bald spots linking
suggestions of a path
slithering downhill to the beach
were there, even though
that whole landscape had been
junked—scorched rocks
around abandoned campfire sites,
dead fish, tires flunked,
stranded on the beach,

the sand limp as a cold pancake.
Each can of Black Label I pried out
puckered, spit.
                    I now admit
that when I breathed
I love you in your ear,
I didn't mean it.
No wonder that by midnight
you wouldn't speak to me
but huddled there, teeth rattling,
your comb snagging, snapping
as you ripped sand from your hair
while I busied myself pissing
in the bushes, breaking
one-way bottles to keep warm.
                    Ginny,
whose face I knew I'd never see again—
now I think we can afford no more
to leave for junk our summer jobs
or any night like that
than to deny these
seedy little deaths we're party to.
On back roads, wherever
ruts turn off into the trees,
we must always come
upon this sudden evidence
of civilization,
these small, charred cities,
glass glinting in the rubble,
the places we have been.

III

Tea and Sympathy

Quod Erat Demonstrandum

All beauty begins with geometry. This is to say, simply, that it begins in imagination. Points, lines, circles—things that we refer to matter-of-factly—do not exist. The "plane" that a running back "breaks" when he scores a touchdown does not exist. It is ideal. The "strike zone" in baseball does not exist. The move of the knight, in the game of chess, is an invention: one diagonal square plus one "straight" square forward or vice versa. The late poet Richard Hugo was poignantly conscious of the geometrical basis of beauty when he began his poem "From Altitude, the Diamonds":

> You can always spot them, even from high up,
> the brown bulged out trying to make a circle
> of a square, the green square inside the brown,
> inside the green the brown circle you know is mound
> and the big outside green rounded off by a round line
> you know is fence. And no one playing.

To change the terms only slightly: the itch to play tennis is the aesthetic impulse that is the basis of all art. It is triggered by the beauty of an abstract idea, of a structure against which one is invited to measure oneself and thereby to define oneself. Like baseball or poetry, like carpentry or mathematics or music or even love, tennis is an art.

The art of tennis might be called the art of "Applied Geometry." Anybody who has played much singles knows what it teaches: how to wangle or force a geometrical advantage from

From the *Iowa Review*, Winter 1993, 5–17.

your opponent and, in one quick prying motion, like breaking somebody's arm, *use* it. Except nobody gets physically injured. It's like feeling out with the tip of a wrecking bar, a crack, a point of leverage, digging into this crack and yanking to complete an idea. First comes the idea; then must come its physical embodiment. The idea alone, though beautiful, is easy. But though it is easy—in fact *because* it is easy—the idea alone is insufficient. Its embodiment is another matter entirely. Though it may look easy to the spectator, the difficulty of its physical enactment is almost indescribable. The poet W.B. Yeats gave this issue a most accurate formulation when, in "Adam's Curse," he wrote:

> I said "a line will take us hours maybe,
> Yet if it does not seem a moment's thought
> Our stitching and unstitching has been naught.
> Better go down upon your marrow bones
> And scrub a kitchen pavement, or break stones
> Like an old pauper in all kinds of weather;
> For to articulate sweet sounds together
> Is to work harder than all these and yet
> Be thought an idler by the noisy set
> Of bankers, schoolmasters, and clergymen
> The martyrs call the world."

Yeats might just as well have been writing about the art of tennis. I still, when stepping onto a tennis court and opening up a can of new tennis balls—*Psssh!*—like pulling the tab on a can of soda pop, sense immediate potential. The balls are so lively they're a family of yellow rabbits trying to tumble from your hand. You stroll out on the court as onto a stage, tuck two of the three rabbits in one pocket, and with a move that's so practiced it's no longer practiced turn, pull the third rabbit out of your hat and with a slight lifting motion release it politely over the net, tame. You're a boy again. The racket is weightless. You can make statements with it. You can reply with it. Everything you see in front of you is a good idea.

❧

In the late 1950s, the sport of tennis was nothing like the sport that it is now. The tennis balls weren't yellow but an anemic white, like medical supplies. Except in St. Louis and Southern California, tennis was marginal, like golf. It was usually associated with country clubs, "field clubs," at least in New Jersey. Those were the days of wooden rackets, and I owned the best racket available, an amber-shaded, laminated Tad Davis Imperial—$28 at Ken Mills Sporting Goods in Morristown.

Morristown High School had three cracked, macadam courts. The courts were slick, threadbare like slate blackboards—three sections of abandoned U.S. 22 across which a net had been stretched. The lines on these courts had been mostly erased through wear and had to be interpolated. Yet even the dim sketches that remained suggested enough geometry to start anybody with a tennis racket leaning left or right, imagining pulling the ball crosscourt or slicing a low liner into the opposite field up the line. Tennis courts are like baseball diamonds or chessboards. Set them down anywhere, and in the midst of traffic, smog, even in the ugly, gray sprawl of a place like New Jersey, a small bright order is established.

The courts on which I learned to play were across town in a public park—Ledgerwood Field. They were called "clay" courts, but they were covered with a layer of greenish sand to the depth of a thumb nail. Wet and rolled, they were the slowest courts I've ever played on. It was on these courts that, after studying books from the library and trying to copy the few players with developed ground-strokes who came to Ledgerwood, my best friend, Pat Burke, and I spent most of our summers between the ages of eleven and fourteen hitting and hitting and hitting and hitting and, sometimes, playing sets.

As with most initiation experiences, I can remember the time when we both, together, began to "get it"—when we began to return the ball to each other without arcing it—our strokes started to look the way strokes were supposed to look: time after time they barely cleared the net. I had learned how to keep the ball low on a single afternoon—it was like a revelation—when I discovered that if I positioned myself so that the incoming bounce had begun to drop slightly below my knees, and I hit it hard with my forehand (like throwing a baseball sidearm, the book said), I could rip it.

Simply keeping the ball low and flat and returning it without error is addictive, the pleasure of it is so immediate, the rhythm into which one has fallen so compelling. *Whock!* . . . *Whock!* Suddenly, in our white shorts, our seriousness, we knew that we looked like men who knew what they were doing, men who had learned all the subtle economics of tennis, picking up a stray ball with one's racket by patting it lightly into life and scooping it up. When Pat's shots were "long," instead of breaking the trance of the rally, I'd drive it back on the volley or the half volley. Formal lessons with a pro can impart expediently the fundamentals of good stroke-production, but for a sense of place and anticipation on a tennis court and for all of the intuitive intangibles like when at the net to pull your racket back because the ball will go out, there is no substitute for experience: thousands, tens of thousands of instances, of homemade "experiments."

In my senior year of high school, I played first singles for the tennis team. To be on the tennis team rather than the football, baseball, or basketball team was almost a dishonor. We were misfits. I was so skinny I looked like I'd escaped from a concentration camp. The Rubenstein boys, Billy and Richard, were overweight and wore glasses. We did not resemble the cocky, crew cut tennis stars with California tans like Tony Trabert. None of us was an athlete or had ever set foot in a country club. None of us had ever had a lesson. Our coach, a kindly, stooped man named Mr. Wickes who taught Shop, played like a retiree playing shuffleboard. Mr. Wickes's advice—good advice, actually—was above all to keep the ball in play.

At the ragtag, public-courts level of tennis ("street tennis") where I found myself, the absence of tennis lessons was sometimes a kind of advantage. I was able to beat players better than myself, because they were locked into a narrow, somewhat snooty tennis decorum. To them, it was better to die honorably than to live like a rat, better to drive handsome but high-risk passing shots into the net than lob; better to try a towering, high-kicking "American twist" second serve than dink it in or, as I did, take a little off while applying some spin. To them it was better to try for glamorous outright winners and barely miss than to let a point develop like a legal argument or a geometrical proof until the concluding step was so obvious that the final stroke wasn't difficult: it was self-evident.

In public-high-school tennis, the strategy was crude—hit it to the guy's backhand and rush the net. Few of my opponents would use drop shots or lobs. I did. It wasn't their geometrical advantages that made them effective so much as their psychological advantages. It is infuriating to lose a point to a drop shot, and even more so to be sent stumbling frantically toward the net to shovel one out of the dust only to have the ball flipped neatly over your head. When, early in a match, my opponent would begin in a loud, whining voice to scold himself in public, I knew that I had all but won.

Our road matches found us in places I would have a hard time finding my way back to, places with names like Bloomfield, East Orange, Elizabeth, Westfield. They were all vaguely in the vicinity of Newark. It wasn't clear whether they were the names of towns, suburbs, or cities. They mushed together: the same pharmacies, Shoprites, package stores, auto showrooms; the same drab, Victorian-looking high schools, the same sooty railway stations along the Erie-Lackawanna Railroad.

Generally, we played in public parks. Some of them were concrete, with wire nets. By the end of a match, the ball would be gray and threadbare. One of our matches took place in a dustbowl. The cranks by which you raise or lower the net were broken. Their ratchets were missing teeth. The net on my court sagged to half the official height. My opponent was a tiny, prim boy—probably a freshman—with an accent that I thought must be Australian. When he hit the ball low, it would stall and slither in puddles of reddish dust. It was impossible to prepare for an orthodox shot. I soon realized that I would have to move up, play almost at half-court to reach his low shots. Our points were ugly. They came in spasms. I began to see that my intention of trying to maintain handsome ground strokes was perverse. It could cost me the first set. Out of frustration, I hit what we used to call a "chop shot"—an ugly stroke with a lot of backspin. It landed in a soft pool of dust and slithered under the boy's racket. He scowled. I began to hit more chop shots. Some of them seemed to speed up, to skid as they landed. Others simply died like slugs, in puddles of reddish powder. The boy would charge them, flail at them, and miss them completely. The boy's primness began to look bitter. I took the second set 6–0. There was no pleasure in it, only a kind of relief not to have lost to a boy whose game was worse than my own. We had not been playing tennis. We'd been playing something else, something without structure, without clear boundaries. It was anarchic, forlorn. There were no line judges, no umpires. Whether a match would be farce or not was entirely up to us. Playing Chatham High, on our own Ledgerwood courts, I encountered a boy who began to call "out" shots of mine that I could see were clearly in. Midway in the first set, he hit a sliced forehand toward the center of the baseline. I prepared to play it. It barely grazed the back of the line. "Deep," I called. He fixed me with a stare of reproach. But he didn't hook me anymore.

One of my ten wins that spring was against a boy named Roger Shepherd, of the Shepherd twins who played first and second singles for Livingston High School. In our first match, Roger had beaten me in straight sets—6–3, 7–5. The loss had left me puzzled. He was so tiny that his serve had no force. It invited one immediately to drive a forcing return. A better player than I was—one with "real" rather than homemade strokes—would have demolished him, 6–0, 6–0. But Roger was a careful player, and his backhand was adequate. I was used to players who would give me points by making mistakes. Bewildered, I watched the match slip away from me so subtly it was over almost before I knew it. How had it happened?

Early in our rematch two weeks later I noticed that the same thing was happening. I wasn't playing badly, yet Roger won the first set 7–5. Toward the end of the set, as Roger, after following the time-honored tactic of hitting it to my backhand, was dancing and feinting the net, I mishit my return. It floated toward Roger, higher than I wished; but as I gathered myself to scuttle for his return, something amazing happened. Roger was racing back to the baseline. The ball had gone clean over his head. I had forgotten how tiny he was. I hurried to the net at once and put his return away.

At around three-thirty my mother arrived to watch. She was joined by my girlfriend, Beth. It was a hot humid afternoon—eighty-five degrees in late April. Roger wasn't coming into the net anymore. I was merely hitting lazy, arcing strokes to him, "moonballs" as they're called now. Occasionally, if one landed near the baseline, it would bounce so high that Roger would have to leap in the air to reach it. It was like playing a midget, Alan Ladd without his platform, without stilts. But Roger was determined.

By around five-thirty, commuters began ambling home across the park. Beth had long since left, bored by such egregiously ugly tennis. The rest of the Livingston team had left. There was only Jaynet, Mr. Wickes, and the Livingston coach waiting for it all to be over. Roger's strokes had completely broken down, and I was rushing the net regularly. I won the final set 6–2. The match had lasted three and a half hours.

I was so exhausted that my very being seemed to ache. Although I had strained no muscles, it felt as though I had somehow hurt myself. I knew this was how Roger Bannister must have felt after the final sprint in the first four-minute mile, collapsing into the arms of his coaches. Dragging myself back across the mown park grass toward the car, past the commuters straggling home with their briefcases, I wondered at myself a little. If *this* was what it took to win, I wasn't sure if it was worth it. This kind of tennis was no longer fun. It was drudgery. At home, alone over the upstairs bathroom toilet, I retched. Nothing came up.

From that time on, in a match play, I recognized immediately those opponents who, like me in a supposedly friendly competition, *had* to win. They were like people dying of starvation, but—and this was what was ludicrous—dying unnecessarily. Their anxiety was perverse. I felt almost sorry for them. I realized that to beat them would be almost like doing them personal injury and that, at some level which they themselves were partly aware of, they actually *banked* on this. They banked on your pity for them. Their desperation was like an odor they gave off that made all my hackles go up. I immediately hated them. They forced you to choose: either inhale the odor of their pain and use it for fuel—hate them back—or play ironically. Unless they were far worse than you were, you had to hate them to beat them.

❧

Even when I was a boy in high school, one of the highest pleasures I could imagine was, someday, to teach my son (That I would have a son I had no doubt!) to play tennis. I had already planned how I would do it. All I'd have to do would be to coax him onto a tennis court, place a racket in his hand, and give him enough instruction—get your racket back beforehand, move toward the ball—so that he could taste what it was like to hit it. A single taste was all it would take. Just one. Whereupon I would float it back to him at an optimum location and velocity. We would start slowly and work up. The aesthetic satisfaction of it would seduce him. The pleasure of hitting was what I wanted him to know. As for the bitterness of competition, I knew more than I wanted to know about that: how it can twist a person. I'd never push him into competition. He could find out about competition for himself.

My seduction of Zack happened exactly as I had planned, in fact better than I had planned. Whereas I had been born fragile and small, Zack had been born normal size and is now over six feet tall. His tennis developed so quickly that, by the time he was fourteen, we both knew that it would hurt his game to hit with me. An indoor tennis facility, Cottonwood Racquet Club, had been built in town. We had joined, and Zachary had taken lessons with the new pro there, a man named David Kosover. Kosover taught Zachary and Zack's tennis buddy Aaron O'Donnell a two-handed backhand so spectacular that when the two boys would be working out together the ringing of their strokes cast a sort of pall over the players on the other two courts, who would keep tabs on them covertly out of the corner of their eyes.

The boys resembled stars. Watching them hit was like watching two strangers. They wore remote expressions. The public decorum of tennis is all understatement—to act as if the spectacular were routine. In the words of Yeats:

> Yet if it does not seem a moment's thought
> Our stitching and unstitching has been naught.

The two boys were thrilling to watch. And they knew it. They were far more beautiful than I had ever been or could ever hope to be. In terms of the geometry of a point, they were absolutely pure, uncompromising. A point was like the solution to a chess opening or a geometrical proof. The queen was the overhead. The rook was the forehand or backhand up the line. The bishops angled crosscourt, and there were always the knights lurking, poised for a drop shot. The court was a clean page of possible lines, a geometry problem, and the final stroke in a point meant QED: Quod Erat Demonstrandum.

❧

When Zack was twelve-going-on-thirteen and just starting his lessons with Kosover, our games were, for a brief moment, equal, but I never challenged him to a set. Even then, he would have been hard for me to beat. I was pretty sure I could, though, by following the drop shop/lob strategy that I had against Roger Shepherd. I didn't. I would have had to try too hard. I would have had to hate him while we played, and he would have smelled it. It would have spoiled everything. It would have introduced to our friendship that same hackle-raising odor, that same despair that I could remember from my high-school matches when I *had* to win. I could remember too well how much it hurt to lose. It would wound him to lose, especially to me. Let other people wound him, but not his father.

We did, once, when Zack was thirteen, while waiting for Aaron to show up at Cottonwood, play out a few "points" without keeping score. I had a nasty spin serve, made all the nastier because I'm left-handed. I tore one in his direction, taking off behind it toward the net. His return was past me before I knew it. He'd handled it effortlessly with his forehand, crosscourt, yards out of my reach. On the deuce court, I spun a better one, to his backhand— like a curveball low and away over the outside corner. He stretched slightly, chipped it up the line. I caught up with it in my backhand corner, chipped it toward the middle of the court—a semilob—and regained position on the center of the baseline. If Zack took my return at the net, he could dispose of it with no effort at all. But for some reason he was still dancing at the baseline. This point could develop into something interesting, into a possible idea. What would he add to it? Zack hesitated, uncoiled with his backhand, sharply crosscourt. The ball dove and slithered, quick as a frog's tongue, it was gone. It was no contest. I found myself giggling. He smiled too, tentatively. We played a few more points. Then Aaron came. I shook Zack's hand. "Wow!" I said, thinking how much I liked being beaten by him.

Around the age of fourteen, Zack began to spend entire summers playing in junior-development tournaments around Kansas and in qualifiers for a league known as the Missouri Valley. The various tennis parents in town got together and carpooled. Watching Zack, with his perfect cracking ground strokes, play in tournaments brought back to me sharply all my years of playing competitive tennis, and I began to derive intense vicarious satisfaction from his victories. I hated his opponents just as blindly as I had hated the kids I used to play in high school, and I relished Zack's decorum on the court, his poker face, how woodenly, insultingly polite he was, and the way he would lean down to accept the first practice ball, the gesture so routine that it looked almost weary. "Some more overheads?" Was there something almost calculated in his willingness to oblige? Was it patronizing?

The spectacle of his confidence seemed to release the spoiled child in me, an imperious, sneering anger at the whole world, a bitterness I'd never known I'd had, because it seemed groundless. What could it go back to? All I could guess was high school. In high school, I knew that I was doomed— cursed with a scrawny body I despised even more than the girls who, watching me as a baseball pitcher, used to screech in chorus, "Hey, Skinny!" During class changeover times, I would slide discreetly like a mouse between clusters of kids, careful to avoid eye contact with the athletes shouting to each other, slamming lockers, trooping up the hall in twos and threes as if they owned the building. It was safest not to be noticed, not to be singled out as different, even though I *was* different. Maybe it went back to an aesthetic arrogance I'd kept guarded like a dirty secret even from myself. Had it been defensive? I thought of the supreme disdain that bellboys and waiters hide from the people whom they are serving, and remembered caddying at the Golf Club in Basking Ridge, New Jersey, how the rich old ladies would address me as if I were a door: "Caddy? Caddy?"

"Yes, Ma'am."

ॐ

My two summers driving Zack around Kansas to various tournaments, fetching and carrying his supplies, keeping him stoked with Big Macs, Whoppers, and fries, and sitting sedately with the other mothers in lawn chairs watching the boys toil in monotonous ninety-five degree heat seemed in many ways a forlorn reprise of my senior year in high school. The quality of the tennis was much higher than in 1959, and the equipment (Zack's three graphite midsize Princes made even my wonderful, old Tad Davis Imperial look and feel like a club) was improved. The balls were no longer a fast-fading white. They were now yellow, or two-color. The boys' attire was shiny. But the marginality of the tennis world seemed, if anything, even more oppressive. Part of this sense of marginality was Kansas itself. The small towns we visited—in which the literal center of social life was either McDonald's or Pizza Hut—seemed, in the faded sunlight and the humidity, almost apparitional, like dilapidated stage sets from another century. But the people were different.

The "higher" one climbs in the *haute bourgeois* world of young people's tennis, the more desperate the competition, the more spoiled and imperious the children seem to be, and the more snooty and ostentatious their parents. When Zack was fifteen, at the height of his tennis development, in one father/son tournament I was his doubles partner. It was Parents' Weekend at the expensive coed prep school that my daughter had been attending. There were eight teams, and Zack and I played a surgeon and his son Seth (a junior) in the first round. Apparently they took the tournament too seriously.

Uniformed like frogmen in glossy nylon warm-up suits, laden down with multiple racquets, they conducted their warm-ups in an edgy, slightly pedantic manner as if all their lives they had to endure playing tennis with people beneath them, who were not in the right club, people who were ignorant of even rudimentary tennis decorum.

At length everybody decided he was ready, and the surgeon tendered his racquet: "*p* or *d*." Zack said "*p*." It was *d*. Zack would receive. I waited tensely at the net. The surgeon served stiffly, a three-quarter-speed spin serve to Zack's backhand, and charged the net. *Crack*. Zack had socked it flat out as hard as he could. Nobody could touch it. Love–fifteen. The surgeon served to me—to my backhand—and started toward the net. I tried to lob it over Seth, but he got a racquet on it and dinked it into the middle of the court. Zack seemed to coast into it. It was gone between the two of them up the middle. By the second game, they had figured out that if they hit it to Zachary, the point would be over. They would have to hit it to me.

It was humiliating to be the weak point of our team. It was like being assigned to right field in grade school. But the humiliation that Seth and his doctor-father were about to suffer was going to be so much greater than mine it would be well worth it. Soon the surgeon had begun, in a peevish voice, to give Seth instructions. "Keep your eye on the ball, Son."

Two strategies had emerged. Theirs: to keep the ball away from Zachary, at all costs. Ours: for me to lob and charge the net. If I couldn't reach their return, I would wait at the net, racket poised, for something from behind me to go whistling past my ear, sending Seth or his father lunging to reach it. By the third or fourth game of the first set, they knew they were going to lose. Seth's thick-lipped, pubescent face had a bland expression that was part resignation, part pout. It seemed to suggest something like, *Aah, fuck it!* Late in the first set, Zack and I were up 5–3, the score was 40–15, and Zack was serving to Seth: set point. Zack's sliced second serve tugged Seth like a marionette into the doubles lane. Seth reached and lobbed it over me. The ball came back past me to Seth again, but it was alarmingly shallow. At midcourt, Seth wound up and pasted it straight at my face. I ducked, then turned automatically to register the result.

"Long," Zack called in the bored voice one uses to indicate a fact that is so obvious, so routine that it might as well go without saying. Seth wasn't so sure. Nor was I.

But that was the set. We took the second one 6–0. Although I've never beaten up another person, it went as I imagine a fight would go between a street fighter and somebody with a black belt. It was totally unfair. While I stood by, Zack dispassionately beat them up. Zack was going to teach them a lesson—a lesson in the aesthetics of Applied Geometry. They wouldn't admit it, but they were going to end up admiring the source of their defeat. He was going to *force* them to admire it against their will. We were going to make them respect Beauty.

Initiation, Shame, Beauty

There are, in general, two ways of knowing. The first way is routine and easy. The second way is beautiful and hard.

The first way of knowing might be epitomized by the way we all learned in high-school algebra the quadratic formula. We memorized it by rote, like the Lord's Prayer or the Pledge of Allegiance and could mumble it to ourselves: "X equals minus B plus or minus the square root of B squared minus four AC all over two A."

The second way of knowing, the hard way, is by rediscovering the process—the story—by which we originally came to such knowledge. This way might be epitomized by how those of us who were interested learned to replay the steps through which the quadratic formula had been derived. The derivation is beautiful. One simply solves the normal form of a quadratic equation, $ax^2 + bx + c = 0$, by the method of completing the square. It's a delightful example of something that Alan once remarked. We were talking about Euclid's famous proof by indirection that the square root of two is an irrational number. With a kind of snicker Alan suggested that Euclid's proof was an example of how, in order to secure a proof, mathematicians were not above "resorting to a kind of low cunning."

The second way, by retracing the formula's derivation, suggests a wider principle: that perhaps *all* knowledge, if it is to retain any intellectual or aesthetic force, must be narrative. Examples of the narrative force of knowledge swarm to mind: the account of the discovery of the structure of DNA in James Watson's *The Double Helix;* Richard Feynman's account of how he first suspected, by means of a kitchen experiment, that it was sharp temperature changes that caused cracking in the 0-rings that brought about the Challenger disaster; Carl Jung's account, in his autobiography *Memories, Dreams, Reflections,* of his discovery of the collective unconscious, prophesying the inevitable defeat of Germany in World War I.

> It was during Advent of the year 1913—December 12, to be exact—that I resolved upon the decisive step. I was sitting at my desk once more, thinking over my fears. Then I let myself drop. Suddenly it was as though the ground literally gave way beneath my feet, and I plunged down into dark depths. I could not fend off a feeling of panic. But then, abruptly, at not too great a depth, I landed on my feet in a soft, sticky mass. I felt great relief. . . . Before me was the entrance to a dark cave, in which stood a dwarf with a leathery skin, as if he were mummified. I squeezed past him through a narrow entrance and waded knee deep through icy water to the other end of the cave where, on a projecting rock, I saw a glowing red crystal. I grasped the stone, lifted it, and discovered a hollow underneath. . . . then I saw that there was running water. In it a corpse floated by, a youth with blond hair and a wound in the head. He was followed by a gigantic black scarab and then by a red, newborn sun, rising up out of the depths of the water.

People who are regular practitioners of serious writing eventually discover that the motivation to write in whatever genre—prose fiction, prose exposition, or verse—is not so much to record a set of received and fully fledged ideas as it is to discover what their ideas might be in the first place, to fledge them, that good writing both describes and is a record of an experiment—the trial-and-error experiment of "finding the right words" for something that, without its adequate verbal formulation, might otherwise have eluded us. It is a way of knowing.

With respect both to the issue of "knowing" and the issue of "derivation," poetry is of particular interest. Of all the genres, the fully achieved dramatic lyric exhibits the most evidence in its structure of how it came to be. To invoke the mathematical analogy again, a good poem, like a mathematical proof, carries with it conspicuous traces of the steps by which it was derived. Its subject matter will always be, to some extent, about its own derivation, its structure. Prose, on the other hand, with its permissions to digress and to elaborate detail, gives an author other advantages, perhaps greater ones. Just as in mathematics addition is the inverse of subtraction, in creative writing the inverse of implication is explication, though a better term would be extrapolation. In this respect, prose is the inverse of poetry. Whereas poetry is an art of implication and ellipsis, of telegraphing context but leaving much nondramatic information implicit in order to display the beauty of structure, prose is an art of digression and elaboration of detail. Prose may be beautiful or not. Beauty is not a primary aim. As a result, the subject matter of prose is likely to encompass ugly facts, whereas the subject matter of poetry obeys a more rigorous decorum. Rarely do we find embarrassing subject matter in poems.

To demonstrate a few of the more far-reaching consequences of this, I ask you to indulge me for a minute while I take an autobiographical poem of mine and turn it back into prose. Instead of displaying the poem first and then "explicating" it, I will try the inverse: I will first present my prose explication as a story—all knowledge is narrative—then I will present the poem that came out of the story.

For me, perhaps the highest pleasure I took in raising my son, Zack, was to initiate him into some of the sports I had loved when I was his age, especially tennis and baseball. I remember buying him his first, official Little League baseball and being agreeably surprised to find that, unlike nearly everything else in the world, you could still, at Wal Mart, buy a baseball for $1.98. Not only that, but Rawlings was a brand name with prestige, a name as traditionally associated with baseballs and baseball mitts as Hillerich and Bradsby is with the Louisville Slugger. How could this be? As I turned the baseball over in my hand, I noticed the label: *Rawlings. Made in Haiti.* It was disappointing, somehow, that something so quintessentially American should be manufactured somewhere else. I'd gotten used to seeing labels like *Made in Japan* and *Made in Taiwan.* But *Haiti?* Haiti was legendary for its poverty and for the repressiveness of its government. If there were a source of cheap labor in the world, it would have to be Haiti. It was shocking how well made this baseball was, too—actually stitched by hand, I imagined, in some sweatshop—a piece of craftmanship, and then shipped to the United States to make sure that American boys like me and now Zack would always have enough baseballs and be able to enjoy such purely luxurious pleasures as fielding grounders and connecting with line drives. This was why imperialism existed—to ensure that such pleasure might be served to oppressors at their convenience and without interruption, served so regularly and politely that the oppressors could take it for granted, remain sublimely ignorant of its human cost. But the oppressors were us.

It was embarrassing to realize this. It is even more embarrassing to state it in public. But what about the poem?

Buying a Baseball

As I turned over in my palm
that glossy little planet
I was going to hand my son
I was wondering how
it could still cost the same
as when I was his age.
Around came the brand:
Rawlings. Made in Haiti.
Like those poor city kids
I'd heard have no idea
that milk came from a cow,
I'd never known before
where baseballs come from.
They were always there
in the stores in bins, stitched
tight as uncracked books,
each with its tiny trademark,
Made in Hell.
We'd test the tough seams
along both fingers' links

to get a thrill of power
remembering how to fake
a staggering grounder out
so it would leap to the mitt
at our convenience,
how that black magic squeezed
in the core would make it
spark off the bat
with a high, nasty *crack*
you could mistake for no
other sound in the world.

The poem is too poised. Its argument is the same as that of the "explication," but it presents the argument too implicitly. It trades off frankness in order to attempt structural beauty, in which the "planet" turns into a baseball, the uncracked book of history becomes the crack of a boy's bat, and the labor by which the ball was "stitched," and the black, voodoo ceremonies of Haitian culture, now exported, have been "squeezed" into an aesthetic "thrill" available "at our convenience." The poem, like the story behind it, dramatizes a kind of initiation, a process of coming into knowledge.

❧

I recall my opening paragraph: *In general, there are two ways of knowing. The first is routine and easy. The second is beautiful and hard.* It's important that the reader not confuse a way of "knowing" that is "hard" with the sentimental notion of "learning something the 'hard' way." By "hard," I mean "difficult," and when I use the word "beautiful" I am referring to art, not life. As Goya's *Horrors of War* etchings show us, beautiful art can be fabricated from hideous scenes.

The primary subjects of the typical dramatic lyric are descriptions of those kinds of experiences that we think of as "initiations"—the first or last time we experienced something that irreversibly changed us: for example, batting for the first time against a pitcher who was throwing so hard you could get hurt; being sexually initiated by an older woman much more aggressively than you found comfortable. For the experience to change you, there must be some fear involved, but not too much.

It's pathetic to have to use my own poetry as material for this argument, but because the only stories I know well enough to talk about, in poems or outside them, are from my own life, I have no choice. The poem below, "Breaking In," was written in 1971, about events (in sections 2, 3 and 4) that had happened ten years before that. The lady in the poem's second section, I'll call her Mrs. Swanger, had been my Art teacher in junior high school. As the poem's title might suggest, the poem is about initiation; but it is also about teaching and being taught, how we cannot be said to understand something until we can successfully teach it to somebody else.

Breaking In

1.
Tall, older than I,
that big kid on the mound
couldn't throw it through a
barn door. The whole barn
would cry, lie
softly down on itself in leaves.
He throws, but I can't see.
I'm just thankful I'm out,
on the bench again,
and only that barn is in pain.

2.
July. The Big Dipper is high.
I'm cold without my clothes.
I want to cover myself
with the blanket, but I can't.
She's older than I.
I hold one of her breasts
in my hand. It's dry
like a hornets' nest.
Why does she cry?

3.
The bat's too big for Eric.
I have to move up,
throw underhand. He
wallows at it, falls. The grass
nestles up to his ears. "Nice
try!" I call. And he picks himself
up. He believes me.

4.
She unhooks her bra. It
falls. Now she's all
there, as exposed to the air
as a raw, freshly skinned potato,
tremblingly earnest, out of
breath—not because she's
hot but because she's
never done this before. She
loves me. She's scared.
I'll have to hold her, try
and warm her slowly
slowly   slowly.

The poem "Breaking In" contains one lie. Mrs. Swanger didn't decorously "cry." The decorum of poetic convention—like that of commercial cinema—tends to prettify life. To describe the scene in prose, though, is to view it in a much franker light.

Because I was supposedly bright, Mrs. Swanger had taken a special interest in me. In her relentless intellectual curiosity—her unusual ability to combine scientific and artistic sophistication—Mrs. Swanger was a Faustian character, and she knew it. She took it for granted that she was superior to most of the women around her and, except for my father's Bell labs colleagues, who were geniuses, superior to most men.

An introverted person, she had never acquired the standard social amenities. In fact, she was not much interested in people at all. She was interested in ideas. At parties, she played the role of student, ready to examine any issue from the ground up innocently as if encountering it for the first time. To other adults, her air of innocence seemed feigned, pretentious, and, as she directed her great corpuscled eyes at a man and launched into a discourse about the refraction of light or the woodcuts of Edvard Munch, all artifice. She must have terrified every other woman in the room. To the wives, she looked cunning; but her lack of social decorum sprang not from some sexually predatory cunning but from ineptitude. She didn't have anything else to talk about, not to most adults. Like a great many teachers, Mrs. Swanger was a true eccentric, comfortable only in the presence of young people.

When, in the summer of 1961, home from my sophomore year in college, I decided to commute daily on the Lackawanna from Madison to New York to take a course in life drawing with Thomas Fogarty, at the Art Students' League, Mrs. Swanger encouraged me. I had decided that I was going to be a painter, and all that summer, on the smoky haul from Madison, New Jersey, to Hoboken and back, I sketched the backs of commuters.

One hot July evening that summer, Mrs. Swanger agreed to meet me in Washington Square Park. Since January, I had been daydreaming about her. She'd invited me to spend New Year's Eve with her and her husband, a balding pharmacist much older than she. A mistletoe had been strategically placed near the couch where I was sitting, and at the stroke of midnight, Mrs. Swanger had approached me in a businesslike way, leaned down and kissed me with her mouth slightly open. Her kiss had lingered a bit longer than necessary.

Mrs. Swanger found me alone on a bench, and we sat there, not knowing what to say. I put my hand on the back of hers and wondered what would happen. She turned her hand over and opened it to mine. I blurted:

"Do you know how much I want you?" My voice sounded ludicrous to me, like somebody reciting a bad line in a movie and reciting it badly.

"How much," she said quietly.

"*Very* much." It sounded lame.

She spoke then in a voice that was both oracular and sad: "I've been waiting a long time."

Instantly we were on our feet. The trip from Greenwich Village back to suburban New Jersey would take an hour and a half. It was after midnight when we arrived at my parents' house and clamored out of her Ford into the loud suspense of a summer evening. We kissed fumblingly, grabbed an army blanket and rushed into the woods, following a bridle path uphill to Remsens' field, where we stripped and hugged against the night air, which was cooler than I'd reckoned on. There were goose pimples on my arms, the blanket was scratchy, among the bleeps of the fireflies there were mosquitoes, and under the blanket rocks.

Her body was lanky, ribbed like a boy's, and in the faint starlight the aureoles around her nipples were nearly black. I was shivering. She grabbed my penis and began to pump it roughly, furiously. I hoped she would take it in her mouth. Instead, she rolled on top of me and began grunting, grinding her crotch against me. My tongue was in her mouth, and she was biting it as she ground against me. She was biting harder. The pain was unimaginable. Had she bitten my tongue off? She was gasping—at the peak of my pain she had come—and now (thank god) she'd released me.

Friends of mine to whom I've shown the narrative above are disgusted. Why, they ask, would anybody want to write this? I'm not sure, myself. The impulse behind my account isn't confessional. If anything, the event was grotesque rather than sad: It was comic rather than tragic. It was almost grim, but not quite; for nobody got hurt. Though obviously misguided, Mrs. Swanger's intentions, like those of the headmaster's wife played by Deborah Kerr in the movie *Tea and Sympathy*, had been motivated partly by generosity. We parted friends. More to the point, perhaps, the fiasco that I describe taught me something. Indeed, I think of it as a *typical* sexual fiasco, and I have a hard time imagining anybody who has not undergone *some* kind of a sexual fiasco or other and who wouldn't therefore recognize in my experience some element in theirs.

The story behind the poem "Breaking In" is cautionary. It illustrates how an initiation may be traumatic if the would-be initiate isn't ready, but how one can learn—from one's own mistakes and from the mistakes of others—the importance of proper timing. For me, looking back more than thirty years, the most significant phrase in the poem is in the first section: "but I can't see." To "see," in context, means to catch a glimpse however fleetingly of oneself in action. The self—who we are—is not, as Jung maintained, a "seed" that is sui generis and that appears only in the four-folded symbols in certain dreams. The self exists in history. It has personality, style. It reveals itself through process, through action—in the form of a story. Who you are is defined by what you do, and this fact constitutes the very ground of the motive to write: to "see" oneself "seeing" oneself. In its very structure, the dramatic lyric tries to present an exact model of such a process. But was I changed by Mrs. Swanger's initiation irreversibly? Of course I was.

That same summer, Mrs. Swanger (I learned later) tried to seduce my brother, and she tried to seduce my father. Who could blame her? She was thirty-five years old, bored, and mired in a dead marriage with a much older man who couldn't interest her. Her energy was boundless. So was her mind. So she decided to amuse herself and, if she were lucky, to save herself. Which she soon did.

Through the contacts at the Bell labs, she met some of the best scientists in the world. Many of these scientists had led eccentric lives as teenagers. They had been, like Alan, geeks, bookworms. They had never been through a normal adolescence. Now, famous, rich, world-travelers, many of them decided a bit cold-bloodedly to make up for the loss, for the youth they had never had time to have. William Shockley, as he was about to win the Nobel Prize for inventing the transistor, took up rock climbing and bought a Jaguar two-seater. For several years, every Thanksgiving at my house, after Thanksgiving dinner, he would show us slides of himself posing in sunglasses alongside one of the famous mountain climbers in the best-seller *Anapurna*. After that, he would treat us kids to a zip around the bends of the Great Swamp, in his two-seater. As I was entering high school, he dumped his wife, Jeanne, and moved to Stanford with another woman.

Mrs. Swanger dumped her husband, trading him in for a

physicist, P, who had been eminent in the Manhattan Project. Alan remarked to me grimly, years later, after Mrs. Swanger had finally bagged P, that a friend of his at MIT who had watched Mrs. Swanger aggressively woo P concluded sarcastically: *The poor guy never had a chance.*

How was I changed by Mrs. Swanger? She left me disillusioned about all adults. They were like me: hankering, blind, ruthless when necessary, looking out for themselves before all else.

&

If we're lucky, many of our initiations, despite how fearful they were, have had reasonably happy endings. Through them, we learned how, when our own children were to face similar initiations, we might help them to pass from innocence into experience without serious damage. Although Alan was mostly consumed with his work, although I can count on the fingers on one hand the times when, as with his darkly witty remark about the "kind of low cunning" involved in certain mathematical proofs, he actually tried to teach me something, I can remember, myself, the few times when, trying to give urgent advice to my children, I summoned up all of my resources—my imagination and my adrenaline—and knew that they would never forget what I was saying.

I had such a talk with my son Zack when he was eleven, the afternoon before he pitched in his first Little League game. Years later, I wrote a poem about that talk and what happened afterward. The poem, like most poems that describe initiations, had some of the rhythms and repetitions of a ritual. The rhythms weren't premeditated. They were part of the experience itself, even the place in the poem where it makes its "turn." Foreshadowing, turn, discovery: all the material leading up to the turn is, after the turn, the same material but it has been reenvisioned, transformed.

Full Circle
for Alan Nordby Holden (1904–1985)

Scared, I watch my son, eleven, his first
time on the mound, stare in

at the tiny leadoff man.
So tense he's pokerfaced,
Zack's practicing the politician's trick
of looking confident, as if a man
could be substantial just by looking it.
But pitching, I learned young, isn't politics.
In the center of that dusty ring
where, as if under some unremitting examination
by the lights your squirmy shadow's multiplied
by five, faking doesn't work.
The one thing not to do, I told him earlier,
is issue walks. We were playing catch.
I whipped one back. I was talking
as casually as I could, worried
about tonight, but trying to hide it,
to talk seductively, I was talking
in teasy little parables, embroidering them—
about the time I walked eight batters in a row,
about the time I got mad at the umpire
and started to cry—anything to make sure
what help I gave the boy would register
before he'd be alone there on the mound,
out of range. His low fastball stung
my hand. I whipped it back. I told him
how sometimes in the middle of a game
if you get wild you can think about
your stride or where your shoulders face,
you can experiment, correct yourself.
As I talked and threw and talked, we never broke
the easy to-and-fro of pitch and catch,
the more I talked the better
I remembered how. I understood
my own shock when my father used to pause
from his obsessive work to talk to me, to offer—
always shrewdly, at a slight oblique—
what help he could. Zack throws.
The batter takes. Ball one. Ball two. Ball three.
And I prepare myself for the first of many walks.
Zack pauses, on the next pitch eases up.

It's nicked foul. Impassive, Zack waits
for the ball. He delivers easy,
call strike two. If the advice is right
and handed out with style
we never forget the things our fathers say.
They talk directly to our sons,
and our sons can deliver us
our own boyhood back a second time.
The batter whiffs. We live redundantly,
and the second time is better than the first.

I was trembling. I could see now. That afternoon I'd been talking as ingeniously and desperately as if I'd been talking for my life.

Tea and Sympathy

One of the most haunting movies that I can remember from my adolescence was *Tea and Sympathy* (1958). The film is set in a New England boarding school, whose headmaster is a loud, hearty, back-slapping, relentlessly cheery, outdoorsy type—what you might get if you crossed a football coach, a scoutmaster, and a Marine drill sergeant. He's the American version of Rudyard Kipling. His mission is to "turn boys into men," into replicas of himself. To understand this type, one need only remember the Boy Scout Law: "A Scout is trustworthy, loyal, helpful, friendly, courteous, kind, obedient, cheerful, thrifty, brave, clean, and reverent." "Brave, clean, and reverent." These are the qualities of a good German shepherd dog. Such a dog would give his life for his master. Such a man is an unusually good civic leader, but not very sensitive or verbal.

The school in the movie is like Sparta. All but one of the boys has fallen into line. The outcast, played by the actor John Kerr, is a type of the artist. He is sensitive and slightly effeminate. Like Goethe's young Werther, he's the kind of boy who in the 1950s in my high school we called a "longhair." "*We*" called a "longhair." We? The Lone Ranger and Tonto are surrounded by Indians. The Lone Ranger says, "Tonto, what shall we do?" The reply: "What you mean *we?*" It's the most fundamental American joke.

The boy played by Kerr was a character I could identify with all too well. He was like Stephen, who, even in grade

Reprinted from the *Prairie Schooner,* Fall 1995, by permission of the University of Nebraska Press. Copyright © 1995 University of Nebraska Press.

school, had been singled out as different. The gang leader was our fourth-grade teacher, Mrs. Lee. A frosty-haired lady with jowls and age-spots, she was married to a diminutive man named Percy. All her life, I think, she had been hankering after some ideal he-man. When President Truman fired General MacArthur, Mrs. Lee spent the morning lecturing us about what a great man MacArthur was. Truman, she whispered, might be in league with the Communists.

In the movie, the other boys torment Kerr. He's already been branded as a pansy. One of the movie's subtexts is the 1950s' theme of conformity, and in one of its most poignant scenes, Kerr's roommate, the most popular kid in school, tries to show him how to walk correctly, like a man, but Kerr soon quits in exasperation. He just *can't*.

The only person in the entire school who sympathizes with him is the headmaster's wife, played by Deborah Kerr. A pale, fragile-looking redhead and an intellectual, she is downtrodden—little more than a maid for her husband. At night, she lies with her back to him, crying silently. She and Kerr are two kindred spirits trapped in a rah-rah fraternity. As she watches the misery that the boys inflict on Kerr, she wants to intervene. She tries to explain the boy to her husband. He doesn't even listen.

Meanwhile, the heckling and hazing of Kerr has gotten so intense that he's on the edge of cracking up. To save him, she "makes a man of him." In the movie's epiphany, she is touching his cheek. "Years from now," she pleads, "when you write of this—and you will—be kind." Her voice is at once oracular and sad, and we know that she doesn't care if the headmaster finds out. She will eventually leave him. She is going to save Kerr and by saving him begin to save herself.

"Years from now, when you write of this—and you will—be kind." Decorous as the phrasing is, in 1953 it seemed revolutionary to me. Now, over thirty years later, it sounds naive. The notion that a lady could or should help a slightly effeminate boy "become a man" by initiating the boy to her own sexual mysteries is a sentimental lie. It's an interesting lie, though. It reveals, in caricature, the subtly fascistic nature of American middle-class culture in the years of *Ozzie and Harriet* and *Father Knows Best*.

All of Stephen's life, and despite the best psychotherapy that money could buy, despite even several affairs with girls, Stephen was as resolutely bent on being gay as I was on being straight—anything to avoid the stigma of being even suspected of effeminacy. All through high school and even through the first year of college, I pitied him for it and, far too often, would patronize him—if not explicitly then in conversations about him with my parents and some of my friends, suggesting that we would be very kind if we all made allowances for him. Whenever the subject of Stephen came up, I suddenly felt quite moral and grown-up. It felt suddenly quite good simply to wear a navy crew cut, to tell jokes about Amos and Andy, and the one about the "homo" in the bathtub surrounded by a flotilla of bobbing turds: Question: "What's going on?" Answer, proudly, mincing with a conspicuous Liberace lisp: "Theeth are my children." It felt better to talk and think like a swine than with sensitivity. To be a swine seemed almost honorable—the choice of a mature, adult outlook over childish self-indulgence.

ॐ

From the earliest childhood, Stephen had been different from me. Born a few minutes before me, according to our mother, he emerged head first. I followed him, feet first. Stephen turned out to be right-handed, I turned out to be a southpaw. Stephen never learned to throw correctly "like a man." He threw "like a girl," a distinction that would be ludicrous anywhere in the world except in America. The distinction is, of course, outrageously false. Watching the College Women's Softball Championships in Boulder, Colorado, I've seen countless women throw harder than most men can, harder than I ever could (and I used to have a decent arm). But the stereotypes run deep.

When I was teaching in a squalid boys' preparatory school in West Orange, New Jersey, the white-haired headmaster, George Douglas Hofe, convened a special assembly where two New Jersey state troopers had been invited, like Starsky and Hutch, to recruit students and talk about the nature of their profession. The year was 1966, and the Vietnam War was in full swing. The troopers held 120 boys of Carteret School rapt. They talked breezily about the virtue of "intestinal fortitude." The younger of the two explained, "One of the first tests we give is, we hand the applicant a baseball. Can you throw this? We watch how he throws. If you can throw a baseball, you can throw a punch." The boys were awed. The troopers were confirming everything that the boys had seen on television. It was real; cops really *were* tough.

I sat silent. The only reason why I was teaching mathematics at this school was because it afforded me an "occupational deferment" from the draft. As Hofe, who was prowar, had beamed, presenting me a carbon copy of the letter he'd written to the local draft board, "We wouldn't want you to be cannon fodder, Holden."

Stephen had actually appeared for his physical. On the medical questionnaire, he had indicated that he was homosexual and, after a brief interview with an army psychologist, was released.

&

I'm not sure when or how it was that I first decided that I should practice being as unlike Stephen as possible. Not all identical twins decide that. At Oberlin, the Loesch twins, William and Robert, two mild and generous guys, were almost as inseparable as they were indistinguishable. Both later became ministers. Their ministries are both in Massachusetts, and they are not far apart.

Stephen and I, on the other hand, competed for everything. When serving us orange juice, Jaynet would squint at our two glasses to make sure that the level of juice was exactly the same in each. If it weren't, there would be an argument. It was probably in the third or fourth grade that I began to notice that at recess Stephen and another boy, Chick Hall, preferred to hang out with the girls. Instead of playing baseball, they'd join the girls for "parties" off in the woods around the parking lot, where they would all trade candies.

Though Stephen and Chick hung out with the girls, the other boys left them alone, for they had already singled out a scapecoat—Derek Remsen. Every single recess, Ray "Chee-chee" Frischconnect or Tommy Conger would suddenly exclaim, "Hey, let's git Remsen!" A pack of boys would begin to chase Derek across the parking lot. He'd let out a blood-curdling falsetto scream. That did it. They'd pile on him. I'd watch from the sidelines. I had one single thought: *anything* not to be Remsen. Years later, during the Vietnam War, I wrote a poem about it:

Why We Bombed Haiphong

When I bought bubble gum
to get new baseball cards
the B-52 was everywhere you looked.
In my high school yearbook
the B-52 was voted "Most Popular"
and "Most Likely to Succeed."

The B-52 would give you the finger
from hot cars. It laid rubber,
it spit, it went around in gangs,
it got its finger wet and sneered
about it. It beat the shit
out of fairies.

I remember it used to chase
Derek Remsen around at recess
every day. Caught, he'd scream
like a girl. Then the rest
of us pitched in and hit.

Only once did I pitch in and hit—a light, halfhearted token of a blow. A token. *Anything* not to be Remsen.

After school and on weekends, I'd play touch football and hours of a pickup baseball game called "inners" with the other neighborhood kids. Stephen would never join us. He spent most afternoons and weekends upstairs in his room listening to the radio, daydreaming of someday being a star. Every Saturday morning, he would tune in to Martin Bloch's *Make Believe Ballroom* on WJZ and tend his chart of the Top 100 Popular Songs. He kept graphs of their progress, like a fever chart. By the age of eleven, Stephen was subscribing to

Billboard and *Variety*. When he wasn't alone upstairs, he was in the kitchen talking with Jaynet.

❧

My family was a paradigm of the type of family that, psychologists assure us, is likely to produce homosexual sons—a family with a distant father and a frustrated, overnurturing mother—only in the case of the Holden family the full weight of Jaynet's pent-up romanticism crashed down on Stephen. Jaynet treated him to tap-dancing lessons, piano lessons, acting lessons. I was left largely alone—doubly so, because Alan could rarely be disturbed from the dining-room table, where he worked on his mathematics and his books. I used the fathers of my boyhood pals as surrogate fathers.

The one time when Jaynet persuaded Alan to play catch with me, I discovered that Alan, like Stephen, couldn't throw a baseball. He threw "like a girl." In fact, Alan may have been, at some time in his life, bisexual. At Harvard, his two closest friends, the late Virgil Thomson and Thomson's longtime lover, the painter Maurice Grosser, were homosexual. I recall once, when Alan was trying to prepare Stephen and me for the coming adjustment to college life, over dinner he related how, at some large outdoor orientation at Harvard, another student sat down beside him, unzipped Father's fly, and put his hand inside his pants, asking carefully, "Do you mind?"

To which Alan replied, "No, I don't mind."

I wondered at the time what this story was intended to illustrate. The virtue of tolerance? Of having an open mind? I couldn't decide. It left me bewildered, thinking, "Why the hell did he do *that*?" and "Why tell *us*?"

In retrospect, I think it may have been out of a combination of arrogance and naïveté. Perhaps Alan was boasting. It was the kind of incident that could easily have happened at Cambridge University among some of Bertrand Russell's circle. There was a tradition of "buggery" among Cambridge intellectuals. But it would have been naïve of Alan to honor it, and even more naive to imagine that it would be of any help to his sons.

Perhaps Alan's story, though seemingly addressed to both

of us, was really addressed to Stephen. By addressing it to both of us, Alan was trying to let Stephen know without embarrassing him by singling him out that he wouldn't hold Stephen's effeminacy against him; though this latter possibility (a charitable one) seems to me unlikely. Alan was not interested enough in us to take the time to be that considerate.

ॐ

Pleasantville Road began to change. When I was in first grade, there had been three families on the road—the Garrities, the Dawsons, the Thompsons. The whole south side of Pleasantville bordering the Great Swamp was pasture. Occasionally a cow would wander out onto the road. It would graze there, blocking the view, suddenly exotic, out of place as a whale. By the time Stephen and I were in fifth grade, the pasture had been replaced by split-levels, and our side—the north side— had more families: the Kendalls, the Cissells, the Emorys, the Pardees, and the Jarvises. The Jarvis family, in retrospect, reminds me of the Glass family in J. D. Salinger's *Franny and Zooey*.

There were three children, Edwinna, Paige, and Frederick. Raven-haired and elegant, Frederick had just graduated from Yale, and was working in New York for a restaurant guide. Frederick had a fair tenor voice and ambitions to sing opera. I remember our family driving into New York to watch him play Don Giovanni in a tiny opera house called the Amato Opera in Greenwich Village. Stephen and I wore matching pale blue summer suits. We were eleven years old. With our twin scrubbed faces, our twin blond crew cuts, we were the picture of innocence. One of the men lounging on a doorstep whistled at us. I had no idea what the whistling meant, but I felt foolish.

In stifling suburban New Jersey, Frederick Jarvis, like William Holden in *Picnic*, was by far the most interesting thing around. He was charming, worldly, dangerous. On sultry July afternoons, when my parents threw lawn parties for their friends, Frederick would orchestrate elaborate croquet games on our lawn. Jaynet and Alan knew that he was homosexual, but out of their penchant for expecting the best of people (and usually seeing their optimism vindicated), they assumed that he would not touch the twins. And he didn't—not until Stephen was eighteen.

Years later when Stephen and I were in college, after Stephen had "come out," Jaynet told me that she had asked Frederick not to touch Stephen. Jaynet was still indignant, and her indignation surprised me. We were no longer children. As she saw it, she had let him into our house, and he had broken his word.

For me, Frederick was a godsend. He would not only play catch with me, but he would let me pitch to him as hard as I could while he announced the play-by-play: "Duke Snider stepping in. There's a ferocious slider in on the hands. Call strike." Sometimes Frederick would pitch to me. He had an arm like Stephen's, but he had mastered a sort of curve ball that actually crept sideways a little, and it was by studying Frederick's creaky curve that I came to understand that a ball would curve away from the axis of its spin. I verified this with Ping-Pong balls.

❧

As Stephen and I were about to enter seventh grade in Harding Township School, my parents decided to send us to a private school. Over the previous two years my grades had declined from As to Cs. On school mornings, I had begun to hunt even the faintest headache down, any excuse not to go to school—not to make more tooth-decay posters for National Tooth-Decay Week, not to learn long division for the third year in a row, not to make color wheels again or learn more about the Four Food Groups ("Our Four Friends"), or mumble the Lord's Prayer, or recite the Pledge of Allegiance to the Flag, or learn all over again about the Three Evils: Communism, Narcotics, and ("when it rears its ugly head") Sex.

The new school, Far Brook, which my parents had learned of by word of mouth, was run by a sort of contemporary Margaret Fuller. Far Brook was steeped in the philosophy of John Dewey's *Art as Experience*, a book that, in turn, harkens back to Emerson's "The American Scholar," presented originally as a lecture at Harvard. In that lecture, Emerson urged his intellectual audience to try to complement their book-learning with hands-on experience in the physical world: one could learn more about sailing by trying to build a boat than from a book. In Dewey's philosophy, the term *experience* is synonymous with empirical *experiment,* though the word experience has now been thoroughly corrupted and attenuated by schools of education into the term *learning experience.*

Far Brook had ducks and vegetable gardens. In many ways, it recalled Brook Farm, that noble, doomed Transcendentalist experiment so exactly dissected in Hawthorne's novel *The Blithedale Romance.* The teachers at Far Brook were not the homogenized, public-school variety brainwashed by schools of education. Eccentric, idealistic, renegade, they were constantly inventing their own curricula.

For three years, from the seventh through the ninth grade, Stephen and I thrived with other sensitive kids in a protective environment, like goldfish in an aquarium where sensitivity was honored, cooed over. The curriculum was oriented almost entirely around art, drama, and music. But there was an air of unreality about it, the knowledge that this world was but a momentary reprieve from the real world: public high school. By the time Stephen and I had to go back, I dreaded it.

We tend to forget great pain, once it is over. My first year of Morristown High School—I was a sophomore—I can't remember very well. I had no friends to speak of. In the change-over time between classes, I tried to remain invisible. Because the school had an advanced college-preparatory track, and because Stephen and I were reasonably smart, we were together in nearly all of our classes.

Stephen made friends. He did it through the Drama Club. Passive, sullen, scared, I watched his life from a safe distance. I watched it with envy but also with disapproval. The girls in the Drama Club were beautiful and sensitive. They liked Stephen. I couldn't understand why. He didn't lust after them. The peers he hankered after were boys. Occasionally Stephen would marvel to me about the "physique" of Walt Morris, Tom Hays, Buddy Kopp. I listened with pitying interest and compassion. Both Stephen and I had been born scrawny, but Stephen had begun to lift barbells, and was acquiring shoulders. I had the shoulderless carcass of a chicken. I was the classic "125-pound weakling" who gets sand kicked in his face on the beach. I desired a handsome body, but I found Stephen's vanity about his body unmanly. In my patronizing view of Stephen, I believed that his popularity might not be in his best interest. I was sure that some of the boys in our class, like dogs smelling fear, could sense Stephen's difference and his fear of them. It was, of course, my own fear of them that I attributed to Stephen. Tom Hays, the captain of the swim team—a guy voted in the yearbook as having "nicest smile" and whose motto in the yearbook was "How's your grapes"—would occasionally coo to Stephen in falsetto: "*Ste*-phen! Steeee-vie!" My only thought at such times was "Anything not to be Stephen." Being anonymous was worth it: it was preferable to terror. Stephen should have the good sense to try to learn to walk and throw correctly.

ᘓᕁ

Stephen went to Yale, I went to Oberlin. We exchanged letters. We both had ambitions of writing and publishing poetry, but Stephen's talent for poetry was prodigal. He began sending me some of his fledgling poems. Their surface sophistication had a kind of authority that I knew immediately I could never attain.

> Vogh Gogh beat his temples
> Till his mind was clotted with magenta spectres,
> Till the anthem soared to supersonic pitch.

I showed it to the editor of the *The Yoeman,* Oberlin's student literary magazine. He wanted to publish it.

Stephen wrote me about two of his friends in Timothy Dwight College, both from California, Tom Mankowitz and somebody named Chip. He idolized them. Then, in the middle of the fall semester, Stephen suffered what must have been a sort of nervous breakdown. He refused to leave his room. Jaynet and Alan located a psychoanalyst on Park Avenue, and Stephen began seeing Zira DeFries regularly. I had almost immediately found my girlfriend, Georgia. We huddled together, chain-smoking, playing bridge, talking about existentialism, necking on fire escapes, necking in the alcoves of buildings, petting on army blankets in moonlit orchards, ceaselessly searching for any place to be alone together.

In the spring, I played on the tennis team. I was seventh. I was chain-smoking unfiltered Camels and, to perfect my Left Bank, existentialist, and Spanish Civil War–veteran affectations, wearing my army surplus jacket. One noon, as I was sitting in the snack bar necking with Georgia, the matronly woman who tended the grill left her station and approached us, scolding us for such behavior.

I squinted up at her and suggested archly, "Why don't you shut up?" I released a doughnut of smoke lazily in the direction of her face.

The following afternoon, the Dean of Men, who assisted as tennis coach, approached me: "I've had a complaint about you, Jon."

In my own, spoiled, passive-aggressive way, I was going to pieces too.

ૐ

Late in the spring semester, the director of a summer camp named Camp Roosevelt advertised in the classified section of the Oberlin student newspaper for somebody who could direct their tennis program. I applied for the job, and the director, Bill Lorimer, drove to Oberlin from where he lived in Shaker Heights to have a look at me. We stroked a few tennis balls to each other, and he decided that I would do.

I was pleased. I'd never had a summer job before. In previous summers, Jaynet had created jobs for Stephen and me. On my parents' seven acres, there was plenty to do: mowing lawns, mowing the fields around the house and raking up the hay, clearing brush from the woods. But it didn't feel like real work, working for one's mother. It was an admission of defeat. It made me feel like a baby. Vernon Hull, a local dairy farmer, often hired local boys to buck hay. But the guys he hired were strapping youngsters used to real labor. As I quavered before

Mr. Hull, wondering if he needed any help, I was keenly aware of what a pitiable specimen I presented to him. He said that he already had enough help.

Camp Roosevelt was my first real summer job, and, preparing to leave on a Greyhound bus for the camp (It was in Perry, Ohio, on the shore of Lake Erie), I felt proud of myself, especially because Stephen didn't have a summer job. He was going to have to suffer the dishonor of staying home and working for Mother.

Lorimer had been in the navy, and he ran his camp that way. Many of the other counselors had been in summer camps before, and a few of them were alumni of Camp Roosevelt itself. In addition to teaching tennis, I was in charge of a cabin of "younger intermediates": seven twelve- and thirteen-year-old boys. I was to sit at their table during meals, know the whereabouts of each of them during the day, devise some supervised activity during the slots when they had nothing scheduled, be in attendance during their afternoon rest period, make sure my cabin was absolutely quiet after 9:00 P.M., and, twice a week, stand sentry duty at night while the camp slept. Nearly all the campers were Jewish, from the Squirrel Hill area of Pittsburgh or from the more immediate suburb of Shaker Heights, twenty miles to the west. One of the boys, Freddie Prater, a languid, heavy boy with black curls and cherubic lips, was supposedly a genius.

The camp was perched on the banks of Lake Erie. It was like living next to the ocean, except the air stank. The corpses of fish washed up on the beach and rotted. It was around that time when the Cuyahoga River flowing out of Cleveland's industrial zone had earned the distinction of actually catching fire. It was like the Rhine River. All day, freighters could be glimpsed on the northern horizon, and at night, over the fitful slosh, slosh of the waves, their lights made tiny towns out in the darkness.

From my first moment at camp, in the midst of meeting parents and escorting campers to the storeroom for their bedding and supplies, I was lonely. I missed Georgia, I missed Stephen, and I missed even more the solitude that I had used to covet. Such solitude was impossible at a camp. In the slivers of free time I had, like a soldier shipped overseas, I wrote and waited for letters. Stephen's life on Pleasantville Road sounded as humid and depressing as life at camp: work for Jaynet, my parents' Fourth-of-July party with its great annual croquet game where everybody, getting steadily more red-faced from Alan's tall mint juleps, broke up into teams of two partners, the Kendalls, the Andersons, the Landers, Mrs. Swanger, Paige Jarvis, and, seeking respite from the stinking streets of New York City, Frederick.

At camp, I had some success making up bedtime stories, and because of them my seven younger intermediates looked forward to lights out. But a situation came up that I wasn't sure how to handle. One of the boys, Jimmy Kushner, began kissing some of the other boys, especially Freddie Prater. The boys giggled about it, and Kushner liked the attention it brought him. One afternoon, during quiet time, as some of the boys were roughhousing, Kushner straddled Freddy Prater and began kissing him on the mouth. The other boys giggled. Alan Liffman, a jackal of a kid who, if the food being served was something he particularly liked and he was particularly hungry, would actually make a production of spitting on the meat to discourage the other boys from eating it, announced: "Hey, look! Kushner's a homo!"

It became a sort of feeding frenzy.

"Hey, Kushie-tushie! Lookit Tushie!"

I did nothing to stop them, reasoning that Kushner would have to learn for himself how to behave.

Midway in the summer was visiting day for parents. Several of the fathers, as we parted, edged me aside and, glancing around surreptitiously, pressed a twenty-dollar bill into my hand. "Here's a little cigar money. Keep an eye on my boy." We weren't supposed to accept tips; but to decline them was out of the question.

Late in the afternoon, I found myself confronted by Mr. and Mrs. Kushner and Jimmy, along with Mr. Lorimer. Jimmy had been crying.

The Kushners were livid with indignation. "What's been going on here!" Mrs. Kushner demanded.

I explained that I had decided that the best way to put a

stop to Jimmy's behavior was to let him see for himself what others thought of it.

Lorimer turned to the Kushners. "That may be the way they do things at Oberlin," he explained, "but it's not the way we do things here."

I didn't know what he meant, until the Kushners left. They were taking Jimmy home.

Lorimer turned to me and shook his head sadly. "That may be the way they do things at Oberlin," he repeated, "but why didn't you just give him a good smack?"

I had no answer. Things like the Good Old-Fashioned Spanking, the Swift Kick in the Butt were like the expression "To Make a Man of Him." They were part of a rhetoric so old-fashioned and sentimental it was quaint. I remembered the ending of Kipling's poem, "If":

> If you can fill the unforgiving minute
> With sixty seconds worth of distance run,
> Yours is the Earth and everything that's in it,
> And—which is more—you'll be a Man, my son!

An appropriate line of advertising for a nineteenth-century English boarding school that required many semesters of Latin—the kind of place where stern, snowy-haired pre-cepters disciplined boys with a cane. It was a world I remembered only at graduations, where older men clustered in academic robes and cap and gown, where Patriarchy was visible, where for a moment as the organ rolled one could almost believe in "standards" and in the Old World.

Recessional.

> *Son* I call him—
> such a serious word
> it sobers me to say it—
> as if I'd dropped
> into his arms a weight
> he could not let go—
> the whole, drab encyclopedia
> of *conduct, duty*—

words so obsolete
simply to utter them
would make the afternoon
slow as Latin.
I do not know
myself why, though our fathers
have passed from this world,
I would want one,
why, still, at the graduation
recessional, when the armies
in the chapel organ roll
and the grand old chords
unfurl their scrolls
of dusty laws, I feel
that weight gather
like Rudyard Kipling, brow
thunderous,
and even though I don't
believe in it
I know the urge
to look up to that tall
weather, a coward,
and hear my own small voice
call *Father.*

જ઼

The last day of camp, we spent lugging equipment back to the
storerooms. My friend Paul Raupack, an all-state swimmer
from Buffalo who had directed the swimming program at
camp, said he wanted to show me Buffalo nightlife. We drove
to Buffalo and began barhopping with his buddies. Around
midnight, I began to feel sick and told him to party on, it was
okay, I'd wait in the car. On my way to the car, the parking lot
began to rotate me like a ferris wheel, and for the first time in
my life I puked from booze. I hated puking, yet it seemed
somehow like a significant milestone in my life. Life in the real
world.

The next morning, I decided to surprise my parents. Instead of submitting to the drudgery of a Greyhound bus all

the way back to New Jersey, I would use some of my new-earned money and fly back. I would make a glamorous, unannounced arrival. I sipped a Camel like Laurence Harvey in *Room at the Top*, imagining my return. Earthy, wry, and hungry as Simone Signoret, Georgia would be waiting for my phone call. I would release a contemplative smoke-ring and remark to her about the exigencies of the real world.

The flight back, on a Lockheed Electra, was a mere fifty-eight minutes. It began with spectacular cumulus clouds in the late morning, a corny winter wonderland of snowballs, snowmen, and, off to the northwest, snow forts, entire fortresses with battlements. Then they were becoming jaundiced, fading, and we had dropped into haze and humidity, the hopeless light of New Jersey.

Jaynet was surprised when I called to ask her to pick me up. In 1960, though the actual distance from Newark Airport to Pleasantville Road was about twenty miles, the nearest interstate highway was the New York Thruway. From Pleasantville to Newark Airport took nearly an hour.

Stephen was waiting for me upstairs in his room. I barged up the stairs, a returning veteran bringing Stephen news of the real world. He closed the door hurriedly. He seemed to be brimming with some urgent news of his own. He was aglow with it.

"I'm in love with Frederick!"

His news moved me almost to tears. Suddenly I knew many things I hadn't known that I knew. I said simply and from my heart:

"Oh, that's *wonderful!*" Then we hugged.

Epilogue

Knowing

1.
My son, at eight, would want to save the life
of the plate-eyed deer mouse
the cat occasionally carried home
to tutor for an afternoon.
She'd drop it on the rug, and sock it in the head
till it felt sick and wanted to go home
and wobbled up to the teacher to ask, "Please?
I don't feel well. May I go home?"
But the teacher smiled, "Stop being a sissy,"
and swiped it in the head
until the new pupil was bewildered,
felt sicker in the stomach,
and would've cried except it was too scared,
and the teacher was talking. "Run!" "Stop!"
"Sit down!" "Raise your hand!"
"Shit in your pants!" "Run!"
"Sit down!" "Limp!" "That's it!"
"Break a leg!" "Run!" "That's it!"
"Break your neck!" "Run!"
"Throw up!" "That's it!" She would
encourage it, ration out its hope
till it could be stored
beneath the sofa like a toy
and be counted on to cooperate.
In half an hour it would be released
like a little old man from the hospital.

Gamely, totteringly, he'll venture from cover
out into the light, offer himself again,
hoping that school is over.

2.

Go! The children lined along the sidelines
are shrieking in a way they'd never
shriek over arithmetic
as the differences between fast and slow
widen   and grow   until it's glaring
as a scream, a public obscenity—
All men are *not* created equal—
the truth we must pretend we cannot see,
don't even know about, even
as it's being repeated   louder until
the winners burst lightly through the tape
and are already banking gracefully away
to accept their ribbons
as if they'd known the outcome in advance.

3.

The man and the woman love
to talk when they're making love,
though not all the time.
Sometimes they'll let themselves die
by drowning. Sometimes
they'll watch themselves drown. They don't need
any equipment. No mirror. Only some words.
A code. Protection from spies.
Mmm! Sweetcorn! Equipment,
they laugh, is for the birds,
for the bourgeoisie.
The rest don't know.
They take things—an arm, a shoulder—
literally. Sometimes, during their deaths
and rebirths, the man and the woman
like to watch themselves
as they do it. *As if our bodies*
were a couple of puppies,
she sighs. They marvel:

how the more they do it the more
deeply they love each other.
Then they laugh about how naive
was the boys' belief
that "strange" is attractive, about how
the more deeply they come
to understand the art
or familiarity, the faster
it snowballs, the more they know
the more they want more love.
And the more they know, the more
they know what they know
what they know
of love.

UNDER DISCUSSION
David Lehman, General Editor
Donald Hall, Founding Editor

Volumes in the Under Discussion series collect reviews and essays about individual poets. The series is concerned with contemporary American and English poets about whom the consensus has not yet been formed and the final vote has not been taken. Titles in the series include: